Publication #6 in the '
Series of Outdoor Spo
from TARGET COMM

MW01092467

'01

On Target for

3rd Edition –

TUNING YOUR COMPOUND BOW

*(including Fast Flight cable system
and carbon arrows)*

by Larry Wise

TARGET COMMUNICATIONS CORPORATION
7626 W. Donges Bay Rd.
Mequon, WI 53097

ISBN: 0-913305-15-4

Dedication

To the man who showed me how, took me to tournaments, bought me bows and took me hunting – my Dad.

Acknowledgements:

Many people have given their time and minds to help this book. They are:

Sherwood Schoch, who gave me the basic technical knowledge I needed and an opportunity to pass that knowledge to thousands of archers through seminars.

Tom Jennings, who gave me more technical information on bow design in just a few years than most people learn in a life time.

Norb Mullaney, who provided me with the correct physical explanations for why the compound operates the way it does.

Glenn Helgeland, who, through his understanding of the reader-archer, helped me put the practical knowledge I have into a usuable printed form for anyone who wants to enjoy their bow a little more.

Ginny Haubert, who helped rebuild all of my sentences and place topic sentences in the right paragraphs.

Dennis and **Dot Spancake,** who did most of the photography.

Diana, Jennifer and **Todd,** who put up with me while I wrote this book.

To all of these very special people, I extend a sincere "thanks."

Library Of Congress Cataloging-in-Publication Data

Wise, Larry.
    On target for tuning your compound bow : including fast flight cable system and carbon arrows / by Larry Wise. -- 3rd ed.
    p.   cm. -- (Publication #6 in the "On target" series of outdoor sports publications)
    ISBN 0-913305-15-4 (pbk.)
    1. Bow tuning (Archery)   I. Title.   II. Series: "On target" series; publication no. 6.
GV1189.6.W57   1998
799.3'2–dc21   98-25661
                                                          CIP

Biography: Larry Wise

Born in rural Pennsylvania, Larry was an instant candidate for shooting and hunting of any kind. When Larry was eight years old, his father bought two archery sets, one for Larry and one for himself. Larry began bowhunting for deer at age 12, which is as young as Pennsylvania allows. He's still at it and has taken nearly 40 whitetail deer in Pennsylvania, New York and Michigan.

Bowhunting led to tournament archery, where Larry collected his share of trophies. Over the years, Larry established himself as one of the top professional archers in the country, and today as one of the top coaches. He outright won eight national pro tournaments and tied four times for first place at the prestigious Las Vegas indoor archery tournament, and once at the NFAA national indoor championship. Larry's most impressive statistic is his five professional team championships, three times with Jack Cramer and twice with Ron Walker.

Larry broadened himself by learning and applying a great deal of technical information about the compound bow. In cooperation with archery industry specialists, he began conducting seminars on understanding and tuning the compound bow and has continued these seminars for nearly 20 years. He has conducted more than 500 seminars and shooting demonstrations in 36 states and four foreign countries.

He has coached archers in four foreign countries; is a National Archery Association (NAA) Level 3 coach, and a National Field Archery Association (NFAA) Master Coach.

From 1983 through 1985, Larry was the NFAA Pro Division Chairman; a member of the Jennings Compound Bow staff, 1979-82; Bear Archery staff, 1983-88; Golden Key/Futura staff, 1986-91; Indian Industries/XI Bow Tournament Staff Director and Design Consultant, 1989-1997, and since 1997 design consultant and professional shooter for Golden Eagle Archery/Satellite Broadheads.

Larry has been a book author and magazine columnist 12 years. He is working on his sixth book.

Larry, his wife Diana, daughter Jennifer, and son Todd live in rural Juniata County, Pennsylvania. He bowhunts whitetails on the mountain behind his house. And he enjoys it … even when his son shoots the larger buck!

Forward

To very few archers has been given the ability and dedication necessary to shoot in the same league as Larry Wise. He is a superb tournament archer as well as an ardent and successful bowhunter. But above all else, he is an accomplished teacher. Larry has the ability to communicate to others the knowledge, the experience and the proven techniques that he has accumulated through years of continuous, intense experimentation, practice and execution on both sides of the archery game.

Lacking this degree of skill, I supplement my test work through the use of a shooting machine. Larry Wise *is* a shooting machine. I have enjoyed consulting with him on the fine art of equipment matching and tuning on numerous occasions. I have always come away with some new thought to ponder, some new observation of cause and effect.

In previewing this book of Larry's I have been impressed with his clear, straightforward presentation of the elements of equipment, techniques and basic technical concepts that define the state of the art for successful compound bow shooting today. I recommend it for serious reading by all levels of archery enthusiasts.

Norb Mullaney
Technical Advisor, Archery
Manufacturers & Merchants Organization
and American Archery Council,
and Director of Bow Testing,
Bowhunting World magazine

Contents

Chapter 1

Pretest For Tuning Your Compound Bow

The following list of questions is designed to help you find areas of weakness and areas of strength in your knowledge of tuning compound bows. Read each question carefully and answer true or false. Answer each question from memory; do not get your bow and check anything before answering these questions.

T / F

_____ 1) Most compounds on the market today are of the two-wheel design.

_____ 2) Most compounds shoot best with the lower limb tiller set one-eighth inch less than the top tiller.

_____ 3) The nocking point of a compound bow should be set at one-eighth inch above the level of the arrow rest.

_____ 4) The eccentric wheels of a compound bow have the axle in the center of the wheel.

_____ 5) The compound is most efficient when the draw weight is set near or at the top of it's weight range.

_____ 6) The compound bow shoots best when shot from behind the valley or at the stops.

_____ 7) Cam bows have a wider valley than wheel bows.

_____ 8) Creeping just before releasing an arrow from a compound bow will cause the arrow to fall low.

_____ 9) Placing a shorter string on a compound bow will cause an increase in the peak weight of the bow.

_____ 10) You are shooting your compound bow from the middle of the valley.

After you have completed these questions, turn the page and check your answers.

Answers

#1 is true and #2-9 are false. #10 should be true, but if you are not sure then count it as a wrong answer.

Score Rankings

9-10 correct — Outstanding.
7-8 correct — Knowledgeable.
5-6 correct — Average.
1-4 correct — Just getting started.
0 correct — Read every word in this book, at least twice.

Common Terms You Need To Know

Before you can use this book to your best advantage, you must understand the terminology of the subject. By reading and understanding these important definitions now, you can insure a good understanding of the many aspects of tuning a bow. DON'T SKIP THIS SECTION!!!

Arrow Length: The length of the shaft as measured from the inset of the nock to the end of the shaft, not including the point.

Bare Shaft Testing: The use of nonfletched arrows at close range for adjusting nocking point and plunger stiffness.

Bow Efficiency: The percent of stored energy of a bow which is transferred to the arrow at the time of release.

Bow Sight: A device which can be attached to the handle riser above the arrow rest to hold one or more sight pins.

Brace Height: The perpendicular distance between the bow string and the grip of the handle riser.

Cable Extension: The length of cable which wraps around the eccentric wheel and is attached to the bow string.

Center Shot: The left/right placement of the arrow rest above the center of the grip of the handle riser.

Cushion Plunger: A spring-loaded device mounted through the handle riser against which the side of the arrow rests.

Draw Length Adjustment Brackets: A pylon mounted near the upper and lower ends of the handle riser used to adjust draw length on four-wheel compound bows.

Draw Length: The distance at full draw from the nocking point to the grip is the "true draw length," and the distance at full draw from the nocking point to the side of the bow farthest from the archer is "traditional draw length."

Dynamic Deflection: The amount of limb bend at full draw.

Eccentric Cam: A non-round wheel usually placed at the ends of the limbs and used to cause a decrease in the amount of weight held on the bow string when the bow is at full draw.

Eccentric Wheel: A round wheel usually placed at the ends of the limbs and used to cause a decrease in the amount of weight held on the bow string when the bow is at full draw.

Filament Reinforced Limbs: Compound bow limbs constructed of modern plastic materials and reinforced with filaments which run the entire length of the limb.

Finger Release: The use of one's fingers and a finger protection device such as a tab placed directly on the bow string for the purpose of drawing and releasing.

Force-Draw Curve: The graph created by plotting draw weight (vertical axis) against draw length (horizontal axis) for a bow as it is drawn to full draw.

Four-Wheel Compound: A compound bow with an eccentric wheel attached to each limb tip and an idler wheel attached near the middle of each limb, with cabled connecting each wheel to the opposite idler and a draw length pylon on the opposite end of the handle riser.

Handle Riser: The wood or metal handle section to which the bow limbs are attached.

Let-Off: The amount of weight reduction from peak weight to valley weight or holding weight.

Line Of Maximum Leverage: A straight line drawn from the axle of an eccentric wheel or cam through the center of the wheel or cam to the opposite side.

Multiple Draw Eccentric: An eccentric wheel or cam with two or more slots into which the cable can be placed in order to generate different draw lengths.

Nocking Point: The location on the string at which the nock of the arrow is positioned for drawing and releasing.

Over-Draw Rest: An arrow rest placed between the handle riser and the bow string, enabling the archer to use a shorter-than-normal arrow.

Paper Test: The use of a newspaper picture frame for the purpose of recording the movements of the point end and nock end of an arrow as it leaves the bow.

Peak Weight: The highest weight level achieved during the draw stroke of a bow.

Peep Sight: A small metal or plastic disk, containing a hole, placed in the bow string above the nock of the arrow and used as a rear sight.

Powder Test: The use of white spray powder on the fletched end of an arrow to determine contact between fletching and arrow rest.

Release Aid: A hand-held mechanical device which is temporarily attached to the bow string and used to draw and release the string.

Return Cable: The length of cable which attaches an eccentric wheel to the axle of the opposite wheel.

Shoot-Around Rest: An arrow rest which requires the bottom-most fletch of the arrow to pass to the outside of the support arm of the rest.

Shoot-Through Rest: An arrow rest which requires the bottom-most fletch of the arrow to pass between the support arm of the rest and the handle riser.

Spine: The degree of bend in an arrow shaft caused by a two-pound weight placed in the center of the shaft.

Static Deflection: The degree of limb bend before the bow is drawn. Pre-bend is sometimes used to refer to static deflection.

Stored Energy: The amount of energy contained in the limbs when the bow is at full draw.

Tiller: The perpendicular distance from the string to the point where the limb meets the handle riser.

Two-Wheel Compound: A compound bow having one wheel on each limb tip and a cable system connecting each wheel with the axle of the opposite wheel.

Valley: The point of lowest holding weight on the string reached near full draw on a compound bow.

Wall: The region where rapid weight increase on the string is reached when drawing a compound beyond the valley.

Weight Adjustment Bolt: The bolt placed through the butt end of the limb that attaches the limb to the handle riser and controls the peak weight of the limb system.

Wood Core Limbs: A bow limb constructed of two layers of fiberglass veneer between which a layer of wood laminations is placed.

Chapter 2
Pre-Use Bow Preparation

A: Measuring Your Draw Length

The first major consideration for any archer is the make of compound bow you would like to buy, but **the most important decision, by far, is what draw length you need to buy.** Without the proper knowledge and some expert advice, the novice — and even some experienced archers — have made disastrous mistakes in this area. Knowing your true draw length is as important to your shooting success as knowing your shoe size is to your success at work. When the shoe doesn't fit correctly, you feel miserable and perform poorly until you change it. Same with an improperly fitted bow.

The most accurate method of measuring true draw length is to draw the bow of a friend who is about the same arm length as you. You must consider whether or not you plan to shoot the same style as your friend, i.e., with a release aid or fingers only. Release aids generally act as an extension to your fingers (Fig. 1) and cause the string to be drawn less distance than when drawn using a finger tab (Fig. 2). This difference can be as much as two inches.

With this in mind, draw the bow in the style you plan to use (Fig. 3a & 3b) and try to get comfortable with an anchor. This may take some experimenting if you are a beginning archer. A local dealer or an experienced archer can help at this time.

After you have drawn the bow several times and feel somewhat comfortable, draw again with an arrow in the bow. When you reach the anchor that seems comfortable, have someone mark the arrow adjacent to the rest mounting hole (Fig. 4) in the handle riser. This mark should be directly above the grip where your hand touches the deepest part of the handle. The distance from this mark to the recess in the nock (Fig. 5) is your **true draw**

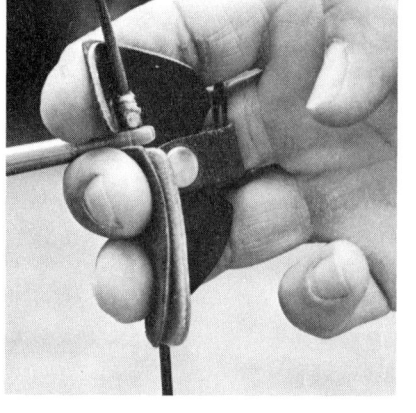 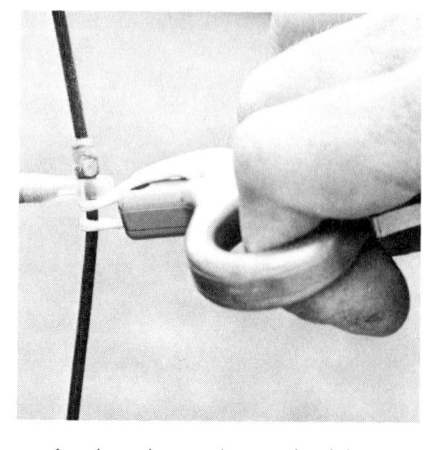

• *Finger style of shooting, Fig. 2, left, requires use of a tab or glove. Release style of shooting, Fig. 1, right, requires a mechanical release which is hooked to the bowstring.*

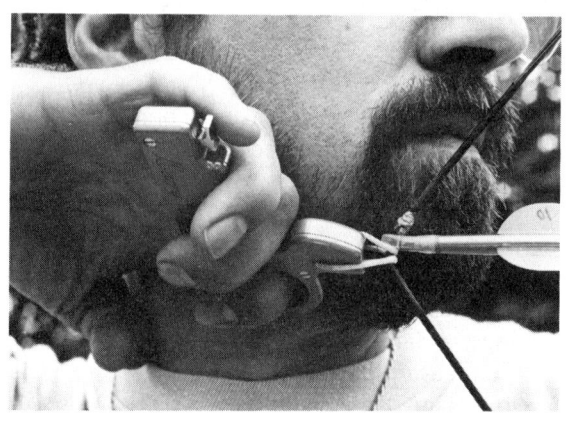

• Your anchor must be comfortable and consistent no matter whether you shoot with fingers or release or where or how you anchor. Figs. 3a, 3b.

Bow Preparation

• *Fig. 4. True draw length can be measured by marking the arrow at the plunger hole.*

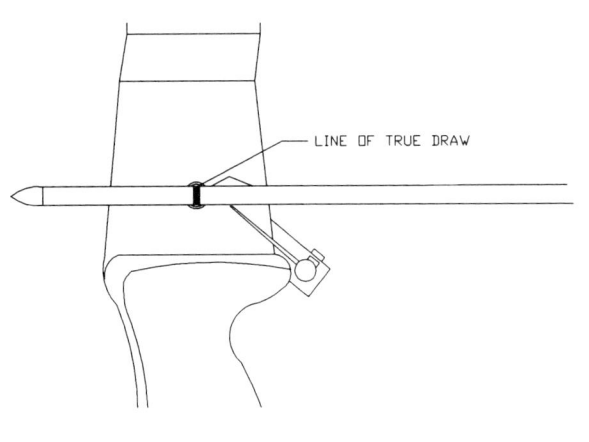

LINE OF TRUE DRAW

• *Fig. 5. True draw length is the distance from the plunger hole or grip area to where the nock meets the string.*

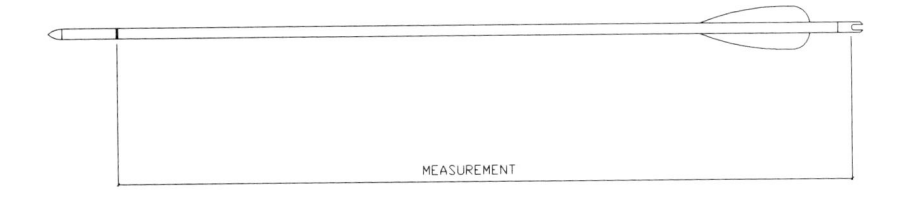

MEASUREMENT

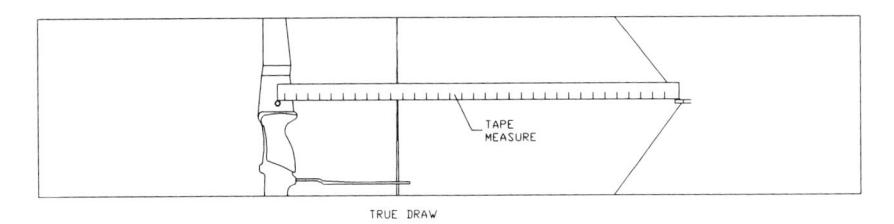

TAPE MEASURE

TRUE DRAW

• *Fig. 6a. True draw length can be measured when the bow is at full draw, above. Below, Fig. 6b. Traditional draw length is measured from the side of the bow opposite the shooter.*

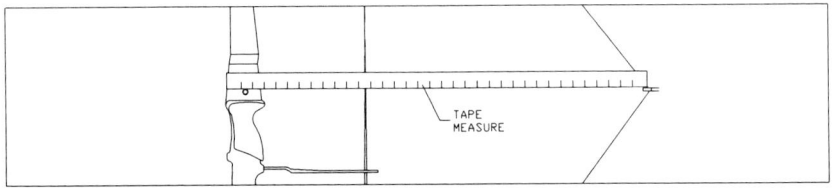

TAPE MEASURE

TRADITIONAL DRAW

• *Figs. 7 & 8. Broadheads and carbon-arrow outserts should not touch the handle riser or the arrow rest. Field and target points should be one-half inch in front of the rest for safety.*

length. It is a measure of your body size for the purpose of drawing a compound bow.

BEWARE! Most bow manufacturers do not advertise or take orders using true draw measurements. Instead they use a traditional draw length which is slightly longer than true draw. The difference is the distance from the plunger hole to the back of the handle riser (Fig 6a & 6b). This adds about 1¾ inches to the true draw measurement. This gives us the following relationship:

Traditional Draw = True Draw + 1¾ Inches

Please keep in mind that your arrow length must be longer than your true draw length so the arrow point extends beyond your arrow rest. How much longer depends upon you and your purpose. If you intend to shoot broadheads, then your arrow length must be longer than the traditional draw length of the bow so the broadhead is not drawn into the handle riser or your fingers (Fig. 7). The tournament arrow must extend only past the rest at full draw (Fig. 8).

B: Rest Selection

Arrow rests come in as many types as there are claims about them. Their manufacturers make many claims about the arrow flight which is supposed to occur and the groups which will cluster in the center of the target when you use their rest. Many of these claims are justified, and many of the rests on the market will work reliably. But, like many other products, not all rests will work well for you. Maybe there is only one style or make of rest that will work well for your bow the way you like to shoot it.

It is not the purpose of this book to look at specific brands of rests. Instead we need to look at **two major types of rests.** For the want of better names I will call them **"shoot-around"** rests and **"shoot through"** rests.

The shoot-around arrow rest requires that the arrow bend around and pass to the left side (for right-handed shooters) of the rest. Since every arrow that

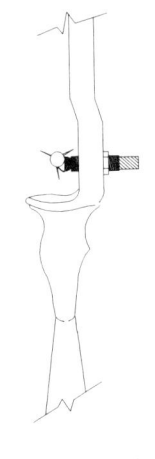

• The shoot-around rest requires the bottom fletch to pass to the side or around the support arm of the rest.

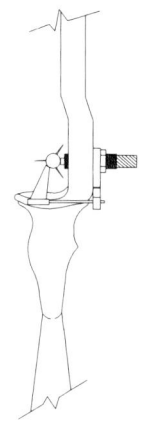

• The shoot-through rest requires the bottom fletch to pass between the support arm and the handle riser.

is shot from a bow must bend, to some degree, through paradox as it passes by the arrow rest, the shoot-around rest is at no great disadvantage.

Some of these brands of rests, however, do not have side tension and down tension which can be controlled. For example, the springy is a single unit rest and cannot be altered, as the cushion plunger can be, to try different tensions for tuning. You can try springy rests of different tensions but sometimes a finer degree of change is desired. Please keep in mind that if one of these rests make good groups for your bow — and you like all other things about it — then that is the rest you should be using. The final deciding factor for any of the equipment you use will be the groups that appear in the target.

The shoot-through type of rest provides support on the side of the arrow and also on the bottom outside of the shaft. This type of rest is better suited for the release aid since most arrows shot by release aids leave the bow with less bending motion (paradox). Most shoot-through rests provide the capability of altering side tension and vertical tension. Either can be adjusted independently of the other, which gives those of us inclined to tinkering a lot to try.

Although the shoot-through rest is my personal choice and has provided my highest scores, it also has some disadvantages. At the top of this list is the fact that most arrows will leave this rest nock-end high. Some archers also have problems with the arrow falling down into the rest prior to the shot.

Arrow rest selection is an ongoing process. Each bow you use may require a different rest to get the best results from it. Your shooting form may change as you practice, and a rest change may be necessary to improve your groups.

No matter what rest you use, you will need to be concerned with its location on the bow. **Arrow rest location is commonly referenced relative to degree of center shot.** Center shot adjustment is the left-right movement of the arrow rest.

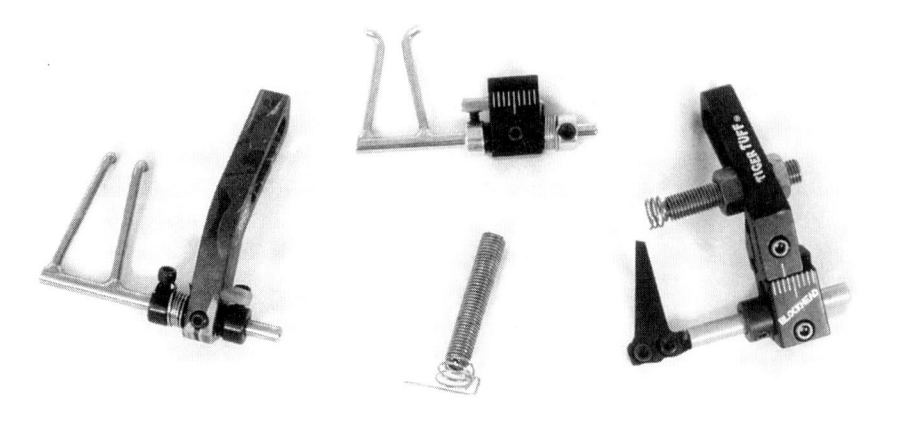

• *The two-pronged, spring-loaded arrow rest (left) is widely used for target and hunting because it bends downward as the arrow passes over it. The spring-loaded rest with the flared prongs (top-center) is great for holding the arrow while you make that nervous shot on a deer. The simple spring coil (bottom-center) is an old favorite because it works well for target arrows, including the newest carbons. A spring steel launcher (right) can be used with a coil or plunger and offers independent tuning of the bottom and side tensions.*

To establish the center of the bow you must rely on the center of the handle riser and not the center of the limbs. The center of the riser is the center of gravity for the bow because of the handle riser weight. The arrow, therefore, tends to travel through this lateral center of pressure. **Generally, the center line runs through the center of the grip section of the riser.**

Center-shot adjustment is one area where the metal riser is far superior to the wood riser. A metal riser can be manufactured away from this center line to allow clear passage of the arrow. The wood riser must be cut with enough material remaining in this center line to maintain adequate handle strength. Remember, the arrow tends to shoot through the center line, and if the handle is in the way a number of tuning problems will result.

Most **finger shooters** I know adjust their rest so that the arrow rides just to the outside of the center line. This enables the arrow, particularly the nock end, to clear the rest while it is bending through paradox on its way past the riser. Begin with this rule of thumb, but don't hesitate to experiment with other positions.

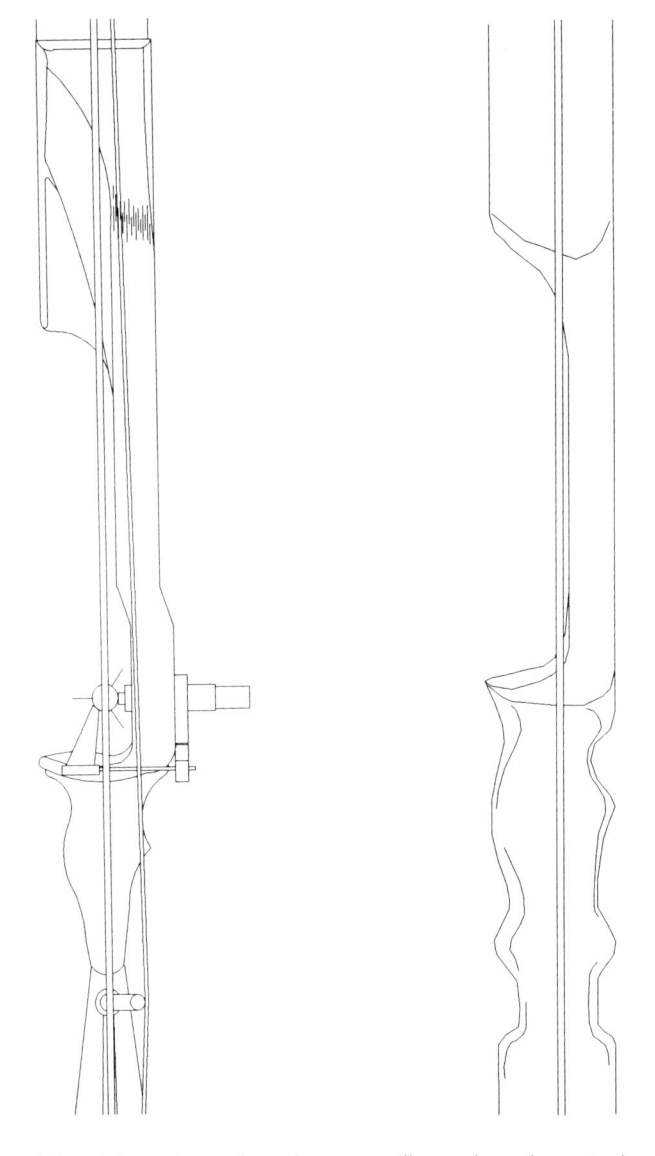

• *The metal riser, left, can be made so the arrow will pass above the center line of the grip. The wood riser, right, must not be cut away over the center of the grip so handle strength is retained.*

The majority of **release aid shooters** position their rest so the arrow is riding directly through the center line of the riser. When shot with a release aid, an arrow tends to bend far less through paradox than an arrow shot with fingers

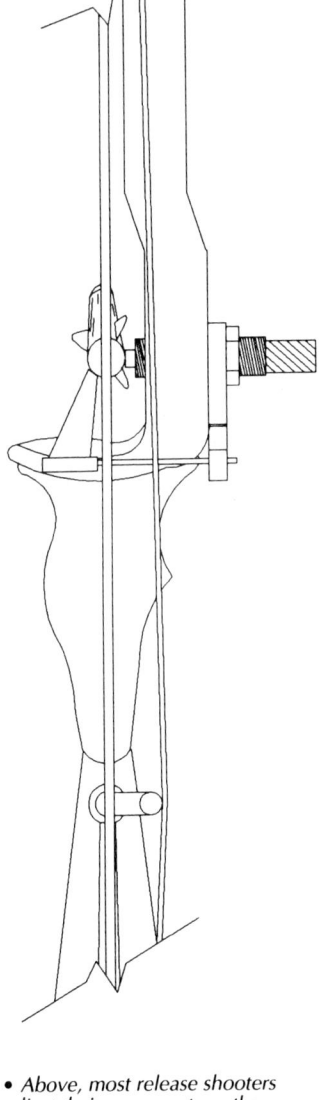

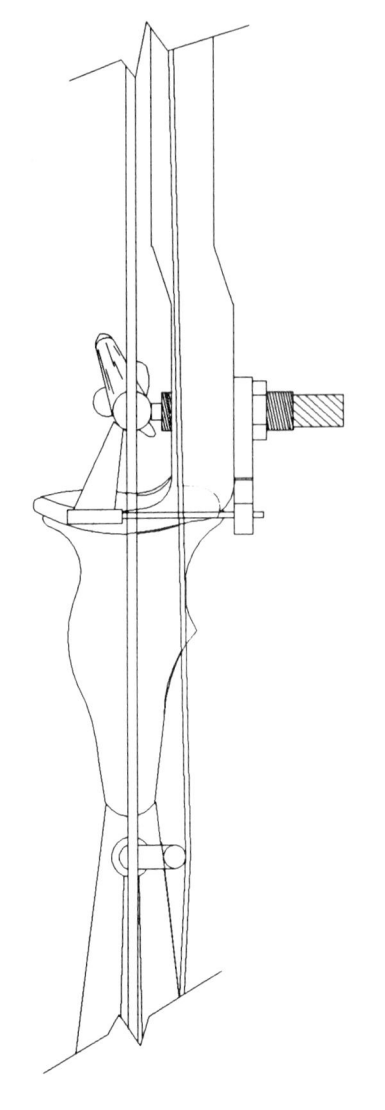

• Above, most release shooters adjust their arrow rests so the arrow is in the center line of the grip, as shown here.

• Above, this drawing shows an arrow resting just to the left (for right hand shooter) or outside of the center line of the grip.

My personal experience with center shot adjustment leads me to the conclusion that little is accomplished by moving it from the positions mentioned above. So, I place my rest accordingly and move on to more important things.

Some thought should be given to the **forward-rearward location of the**

rest. The compound bow riser is designed so the rest is located above or nearly above the pressure point of the grip. Moving the rest forward or rearward of the grip pressure point has the effect of magnifying poor hand position and hand torque. The overdraw rest is the classic example of this situation. Turning or twisting the riser upon release causes a significant left or right movement of the rest relative to the grip and to the sight. The result is an unexpected left or right impact point in the target. Be aware of this condition if you plan to use an overdraw rest assembly.

• The over-draw arrow rest is positioned between the handle riser and the bowstring.

C: Sight Mounting

Installing a bow sight seems to be a simple task, but if not done carefully it can cause many problems. To avoid these problems follow a few simple rules.

The first consideration for bow sight installation is the **condition of the sight mounting holes** placed in the riser by the manufacturer. All burrs and metal pieces should be cleaned from these holes with a hole tap device (Fig.

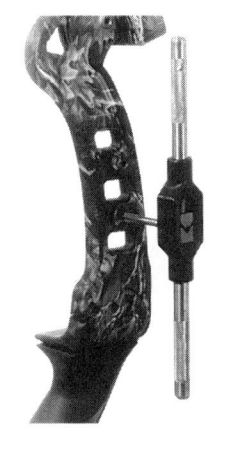

• Fig. 19. Use a thread tap to clean the sight mounting holes.

19). Then the mounting screws should be run in and out of the hole to insure that the threads are working properly. Be sure that the screws are the proper length to hold the sight and the cable guard if your bow needs a guard.

At this time you must be careful not to overtighten the mounting screws and to be sure that the screws are not too long for the hole. Just turning them **snug is all that is necessary;** the aluminum or magnesium handle riser does not provide strong threads for screws and may become stripped if overtightened.

If you plan to use a **tournament sight,** you have several other considerations. After the tournament sight block has been mounted, you must adjust the vertical bar to insure that the sight block will slide in a vertical direction when moving it from one distance to another. A small level comes in handy for this adjustment.

• *Use a carpenter's level to plumb a vertical sight bar.*

Find a door jamb which is plumb (Fig. 20) and place your bow against it so only the sides of the top and bottom limbs touch the jamb. Using the level, adjust the vertical sight bar so that it is plumb. Next, adjust the sight block so the level bubble shows that it is correspondingly level. These steps should satisfy your needs and avoid some problems until we get to the chapter on shoot testing.

If you use a **peep sight** it must also be installed. A simple method of wrapping and knotting serving thread above and below the peep (Fig. 21) can hold it in place and yet allow you to adjust it so it rolls around to your eye, shot after shot. Final location of the peep cannot be determined until after we set the nocking point in a later section.

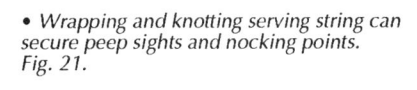

• Wrapping and knotting serving string can secure peep sights and nocking points. Fig. 21.

D: Tiller Adjustment

The tiller of a bow refers to the distance between the string and each limb. This distance on the compound bow is measured at the point where the limb is attached to the handle riser and perpendicular to the string (Fig. 22). Consequently, each limb has its own tiller measurement.

Changing the tiller measurements is not necessary in order to tune the two-wheel compound bow, but it can be effective to a small degree in tuning a four-wheel compound bow.

Most manufacturers bend test each limb and match the top and bottom limbs on a given bow. For this reason, limbs on today's compounds perform near equal amounts of work and are generally well balanced during the power stroke.

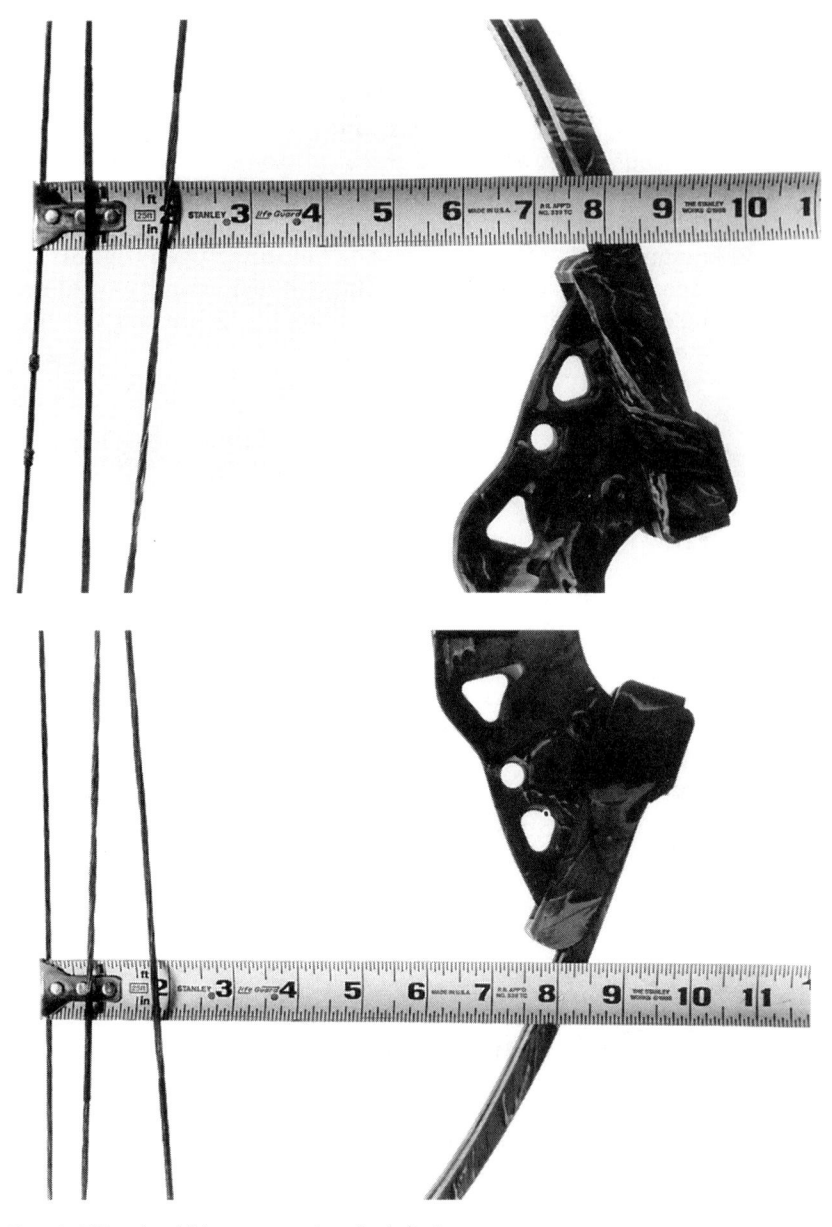

• *Fig. 22. Tiller should be measured on both limbs.*

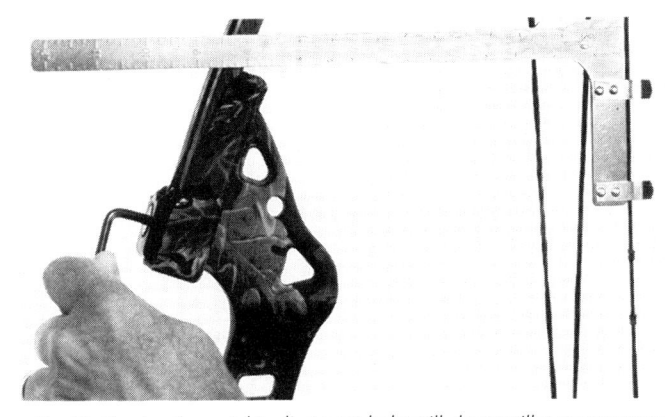

• *Fig. 23. Turning the weight adjustment bolts will change tiller measurements.*

Making tiller adjustments on today's compound bows is an easy task. To decrease the top limb tiller measurement, you need only turn the top limb weight adjustment bolt inward (clockwise) (Fig. 23). To increase the top limb tiller, turn the weight bolt outward (counter-clockwise). The same adjustments can be made to the lower limb tiller. Please remember that **any adjustment to one limb will cause a change in the other limb.**

The **two-wheel compound bow** is a closed circuit system. In other words, the cable system connects each wheel directly to the other wheel. In this closed system the limbs are in constant balance with one another. Turning the weight bolt of one limb cannot make it work more or less than the other limb. By changing the weight bolt of one limb, you only succeed in changing the angle at which the handle riser sits between the two limbs.

The **four-wheel compound,** on the other hand, is not a closed circuit system because neither eccentric wheel is connected directly to the other wheel. The return cable from each eccentric wheel is connected to an idler wheel and then to a draw length adjustment bracket. In the four-wheel cable system, changing the weight bolt of one limb can cause the limb to work more or to work less than the other limb. This weight bolt adjustment or tiller adjustment can also cause a slight change in the timing of eccentric rollover.

Tiller adjustments on the **two-wheel compound** should be made whenever you first adjust the draw weight. To do this, **measure the distance from the string to that point where the limb meets the handle riser, then turn the weight adjustment bolts to obtain the desired measurements.** Most shooters prefer that the top limb tiller be the same as or one-eighth inch more than the bottom limb tiller. Because both limbs will always work equally on a two-wheel bow, it does not matter what your tiller measurements are, but only that you set them and check them regularly to be sure that they haven't changed.

Measuring and setting the tiller measurements on a one-cam bow can be done easily if a string is stretched between the axles and used as a reference line, instead of the bowstring being used as the reference point. For your initial tuning steps, I recommend setting the tiller measurements equal. After that, try some other tiller setting to see if you aim the bow better with one setting than another.

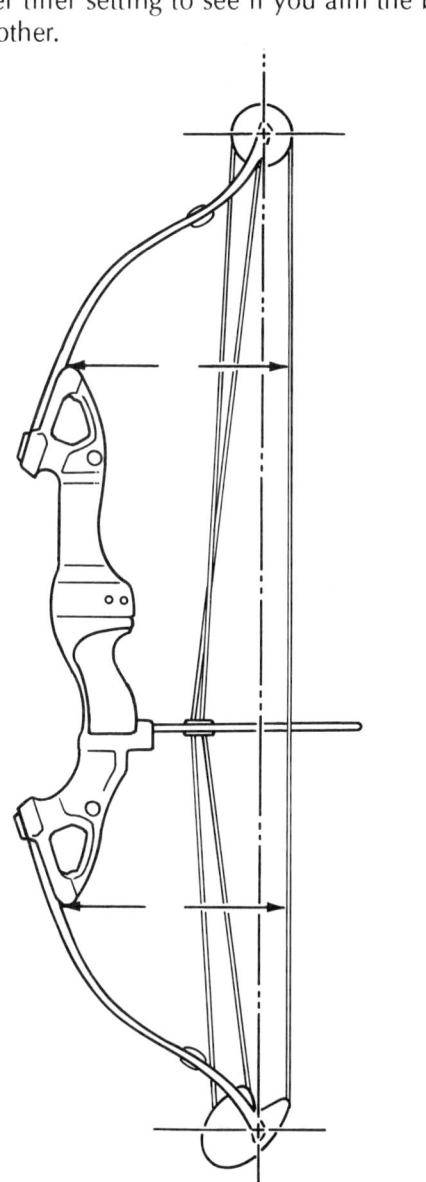

• Set both top and bottom limb tiller measurements equal relative to a string line between axles.

Bow Preparation

E: Draw Weight Adjustment

When the tiller measurements have been set to your satisfaction, the draw weight should be set (Fig. 25). The most common method for setting this

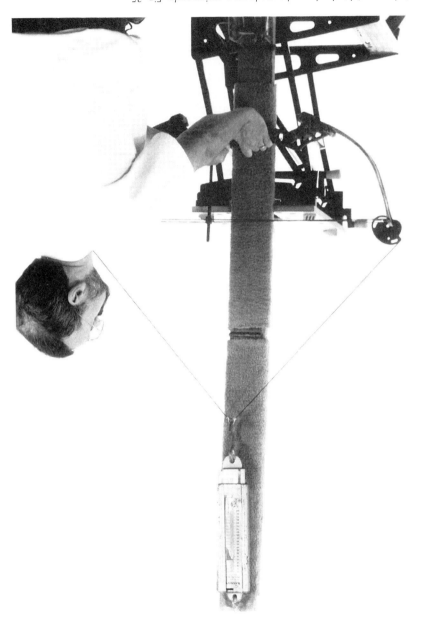

- A draw weight check can be made on a spring scale. Fig. 25.

is to use a spring tension scale. Since the tiller measurements have been established, you should be careful to **adjust the top weight adjustment bolt and the bottom weight bolt the same number of turns.** If they are adjusted the same, then the tiller will be unchanged no matter what the weight. For example, if you set the tiller measurements at equal distances then they will remain equal to one another.

From this point on, both weight adjustment bolts should be turned the same number of turns when changing draw weight. **The amount of weight change per turn is dependent on the wheel size, the pitch of the threads on the adjustment bolts, and the bow's potential peak weight.** The larger the wheel, the more weight change per turn. The heavier the draw weight, the more weight change per turn. As a rule of thumb, a compound with a 28 inch true-draw length will increase about five percent of it's draw weight when the adjustment bolts are turned inward or clockwise one full turn. The bow will lose about five percent of it's draw weight when the bolts are turned counterclockwise one full turn.

When weight adjustments are made with bolts through the butt end of the limbs, then draw length will not be effected to any great degree. Some compounds offer other methods of changing draw weight such as moving idler pulleys which further stress cables. This method of changing draw weight will also change the draw length of your compound. Chapter Three of this book will make clear why you must be very careful when dealing with this model bow.

F: Setting The Nocking Point

When the tiller measurements and the draw weight have been set, then the nocking point can be placed on the string with some degree of reliability. To have put it on before this would have been useless since adjusting the tiller distances would alter its position relative to the arrow rest.

At this point in the tuning of your bow, we need only a starting position for the nocking point. As the tuning process continues, it may become necessary to move the nocking point up or down from its original position. **The recommended starting position should be about one-fourth inch above level (Fig. 26).** This position should allow the bottom of the arrow shaft to be level to or above its resting place on the arrow rest.

To begin with the arrow riding too low may give you some false readings in later tuning steps. Less drastic side effects occur when the arrow is resting too high. Remember that this is **only a starting placement** for the nocking point.

More nock-set rings are probably sold than any other accessory item in archery. They do the job. My only suggestion is to use two of them placed above the nock of the arrow (Fig. 27). This will give you a more secure setting which will be far less likely to slide up or down the string.

Another common method used is that of tying nylon serving thread on the string using single wraps with a knot on alternating sides of the string. Ten wraps is sufficient. Supporting this with a nock set ring is a good idea.

This knotted serving will not dig into nocks or leave marks on nocks and should also turn up and down the serving threads to allow fine adjustment of the nocking point. This type of nocking point should be covered with fletching glue so it becomes hard and durable. You must constantly be looking for adjustability while maintaining durability.

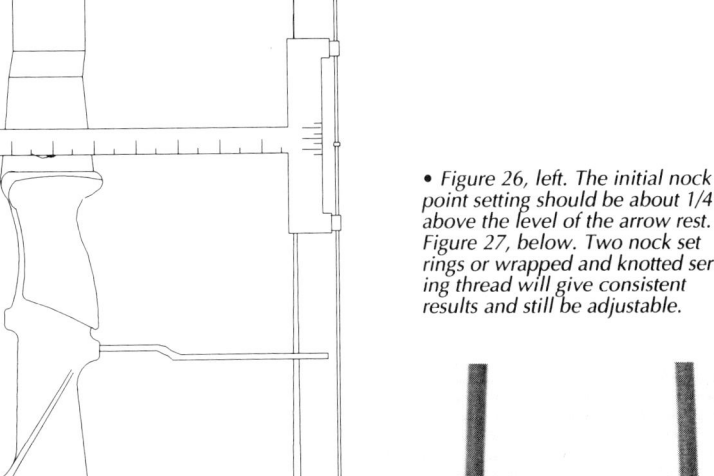

• *Figure 26, left. The initial nock point setting should be about 1/4" above the level of the arrow rest. Figure 27, below. Two nock set rings or wrapped and knotted serving thread will give consistent results and still be adjustable.*

G: Chapter Summary

Patience, archer. You are not yet ready to shoot this creation you have built. **The most important step is yet to come — setting the draw length to your body size.** Before that is done you might want to double check everything we have done to this point.

You should also check for comfort and noise in your bow. Perhaps a small amount of lubrication (Tri Flon is recommended) is needed on the axles. Check to be sure that the wheels and spacers on the axle are not binding. This occurs when too many spacers are placed on the axle. The split limb tips, if your bow is of this design, could be spread apart by too many spacers, causing undue drag and thus poor performance (Fig. 28).

Check to be sure that the axles have clip rings on both ends. Without them you could end your shooting early today while you rounded up the parts.

Take a short break right now. Then when you begin Chapter Three be attentive, because it is the most important chapter in this or any other tuning book! Without Chapter Three everything you do to tune your bow will be without reliability.

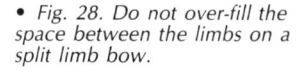

• *Fig. 28. Do not over-fill the space between the limbs on a split limb bow.*

Chapter 3
The Draw Stroke of the Compound Bow

A: The Force-Draw Curve Of The Compound Bow

Do you recall the first time you drew a compound to full draw? If you had always shot a recurve bow or long bow until then, it was a feeling that totally opposed everything you had experienced with a bow. And that first shot seemed to overwhelm you with speed. If you were like I was, I handed the bow back to its owner and looked in awe at the seemingly complicated mass of cables, string and wheels. The question surfaced in my mind very quickly, "How would you ever adjust and tune such a contraption?"

That was August, 1976, for me. Today, I can't remember the last time I flexed a recurve bow. I'm sure the stark contrast in feel would still seem very strange. It is this contrast which is at the heart of what makes a compound bow work.

The feel of the compound bow, which is controlled by the eccentric wheel system, is so essential to good shooting that it becomes the single most important concern when tuning. It is the eccentric wheel system which causes the compound to move through three phases during its draw cycle. If these three phases do not match your draw length, then this desired feel is not correct. And if the bow does not feel good to you and does not fit you, then you will never achieve and maintain the standard of success you have set for yourself.

To understand the **three phases in the draw cycle** of the compound bow you must know some simple technical facts about the eccentric wheel or cam. Only then can you take the first and most important step in tuning the compound bow.

• *Fig. 29. The scale, winch and tape measure are all that is needed to make a force-draw curve of any bow.*

No elaborate equipment is needed to measure this sequence of three phases. A 0-100 pound spring scale and a boat trailer winch are all that are necessary. An arrow marked in eighth inches is also helpful.

Begin by placing the bow string in the scale hook as shown in Figure 29. Fasten the winch rope to the grip section of the bow. Turn the winch handle so the bow is drawn one inch at a time. You can create a graph or picture of how your bow reacts as it is drawn to full draw by measuring and recording the draw weight at each inch.

This graph or **FORCE-DRAW curve** shows the three phases of the compound bow. Moving from left to right, the graph first slopes sharply upward (Fig. 30). This upward swing on the curve represents an increase in draw weight. As the curve reaches its highest point we pass what is termed "peak weight" (Fig. 31). As we continue to the right, the curve slopes downward (Fig. 32) and continues to the valley which is represented on the graph by the bottom of the downward slope (Fig. 33). To the right of the valley the curve swings upward again and the final phase of the draw cycle, the "wall" is represented (Fig. 34).

The area under the force-draw curve represents the amount of energy that has been stored by the limbs of the bow. A large portion of this energy is

• Fig. 30, top left, the first action of the draw stroke of the compound bow is an increase in weight. Fig. 31, middle left, as the bow reaches its maximum weight, the curve peaks. Fig. 32, lower left, after peak weight is reached, the weight on the bowstring decreases. Fig. 33, top right, at the point of lowest force on the string, the curve reaches the valley. Fig. 34, middle right, when drawn beyond the valley, the weight on the string increases rapidly up the wall. Fig. 35, lower right, the force-draw curve of the cam goes up faster in the beginning and stays at peak longer.

transferred to the arrow as the bow is released. How much energy is transferred determines how fast the arrow will travel. For this reason, we're always looking for ways to store more energy in the bow.

One popular method of storing more energy is to use a cam-shaped or non-round wheel. The cam has a slightly different force-draw curve (Fig. 35). The basic idea behind the cam is to make the bow reach peak weight earlier, hold it longer and drop more sharply into the valley. The resulting curve shows more area and, therefore, more stored energy in the bow.

Please remember that you never get anything for nothing in this sport, and so it is with the cam. The increase in stored energy must be put there by the archer as he draws the bow. The cam can be a faster shooting bow but because of the steep increase and the steep decrease in its force-draw curve, it can be somewhat uncomfortable to use.

B: Exploring The Eccentric Wheel

The eccentric wheel system is the heart of the compound bow. It is the action of this wheel which causes the three phases of the draw-force curve. Understanding the mechanics of the eccentric wheel will help explain why these phases occur and ultimately how to adjust these phases to your draw length.

The eccentric wheel, because its axle is not in the center, acts as a lever which has a changing leverage ratio. The **point of maximum leverage** is found by drawing a line from the axle hole of the wheel, through the center of the wheel, to the opposite edge of the wheel (Fig. 36). This line locates that point on the edge of the wheel which is the farthest from the axle hole. Mark this point so its position can be noted during the three phases of the draw cycle.

• Fig. 36. The line of maximum leverage can be drawn from the axle through the center of the wheel to the far side of the wheel.

When the bow is at rest or in the braced position, the maximum leverage line is located near the limb. However, there is no significance in the location of the limb in this position. As you draw the bow toward peak weight, the maximum leverage line rotates toward the end of the limb tips (Fig. 37). As the bow reaches peak weight the line will form a right angle with the tip of the limb (Fig. 38). This is where the leverage ratio between the string

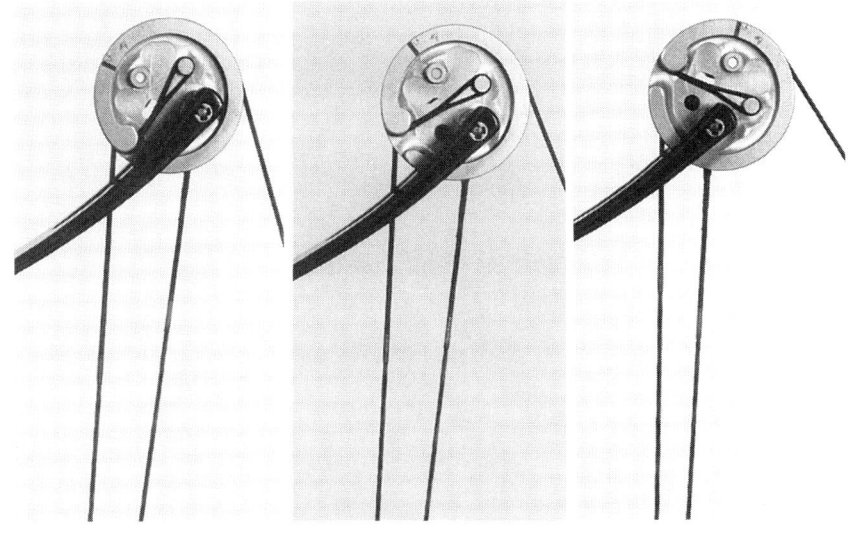

• *Figs. 37, 38, 39, left to right, show the eccentric wheel before reaching peak weight, at peak weight and after passing peak weight. At peak weight, the line of maximum leverage is at right angle to the limb tip.*

and cables reaches a position where the string begins carrying less load (Fig. 39).

This decrease in weight on the string does not continue forever. The diameter of any eccentric is limited in size and therefore will give let-off for a limited distance. **Larger wheels will give let-off over a greater distance than smaller wheels.** Therefore, larger people need larger wheels. As the let-off ends, you reach the "valley" or the point of maximum let-off. Beyond this point in the draw cycle the string will begin to carry more load, and this load will increase very rapidly.

The next three illustrations are the most important part of this book. Figure 40 shows the maximum leverage line just before reaching the valley. Figure 41a shows the maximum leverage line in the middle of the valley and Figure 42 shows the line as the bow passes the valley. Should you continue drawing the bow beyond the middle of the valley, the draw weight will begin to increase very sharply. This increase is so steep that some archers describe it as the "wall." Once the bow is drawn beyond the valley it begins working like a straight-limbed bow — the farther you pull it, the greater the weight becomes.

Review Figure 41a again. The leverage line through the wheel is ending at the point where the string cable is leaving the wheel. The wheel will not give you any mechanical advantage when drawn beyond this point. Therefore, the weight felt on the string has to increase rapidly.

For the best performance, both wheels must be operating on the same force-draw curve. If each wheel is operating on an independent curve, then

Draw Stroke

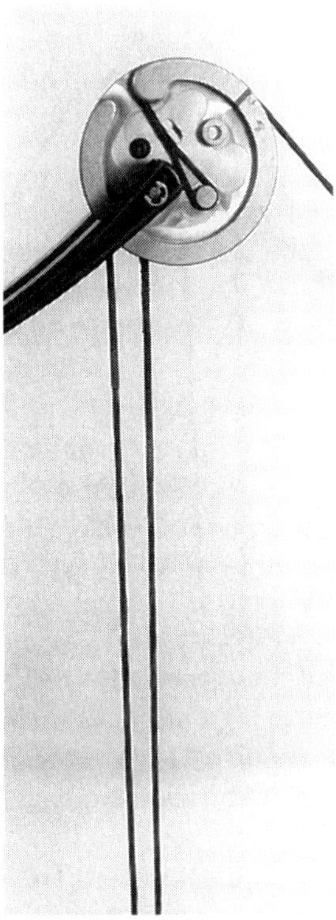

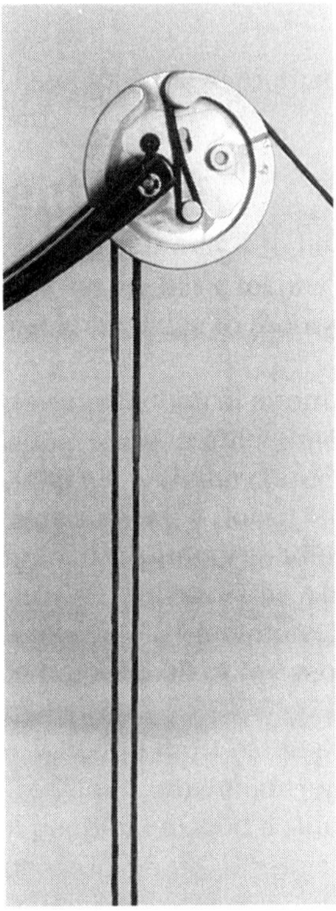

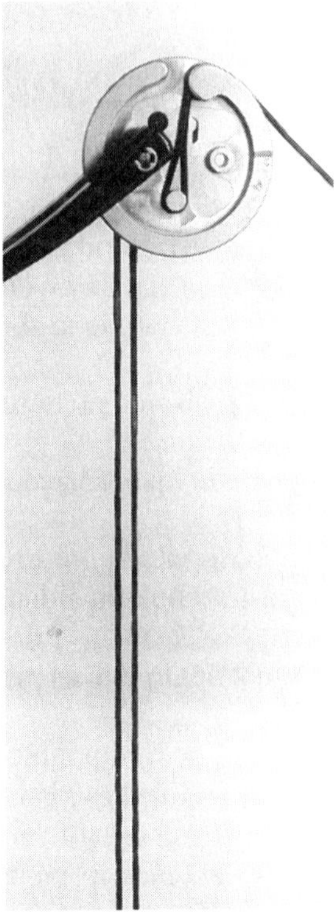

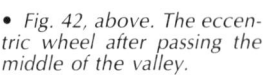

• *Fig. 40, above. The eccentric wheel at the front of the valley.*

• *Figs. 41 a & b, center. When drawn to the middle of the valley, the maximum leverage line points to where the string cable is leaving the wheel. Both wheels — top and bottom limb — should roll the same amount.*

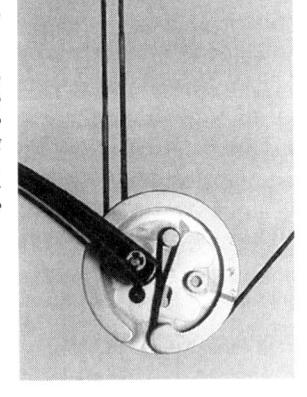

• *Fig. 42, above. The eccentric wheel after passing the middle of the valley.*

poor arrow flight and overall bad performance are the results. This condition is most often found in four-wheel compounds since the roll-over of each wheel can be independently adjusted. Two wheel compounds are built with syncronized roll-over (Fig. 41a and 41b) which is retained as long as the cables do not slip in the eccentrics. Corrections for this condition are discussed in Chapter Four.

Draw Stroke

C: Exploring The Cam

The cam wheel follows the same three basic stages as the round wheel. From the force-draw curve pictured (Fig. 43), you can see the upward slopes and the downward slopes are much steeper and the peak is wider. Although more energy is stored in the limbs by the cam, the valley is usually narrower (Fig. 44).

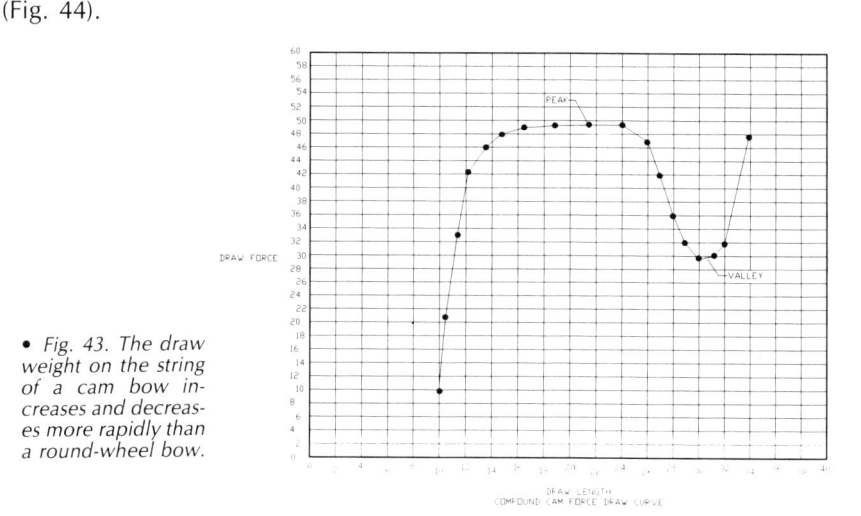

• *Fig. 43. The draw weight on the string of a cam bow increases and decreases more rapidly than a round-wheel bow.*

• *Fig. 44. The valley area on the cam wheel force-draw curve is usually very narrow.*

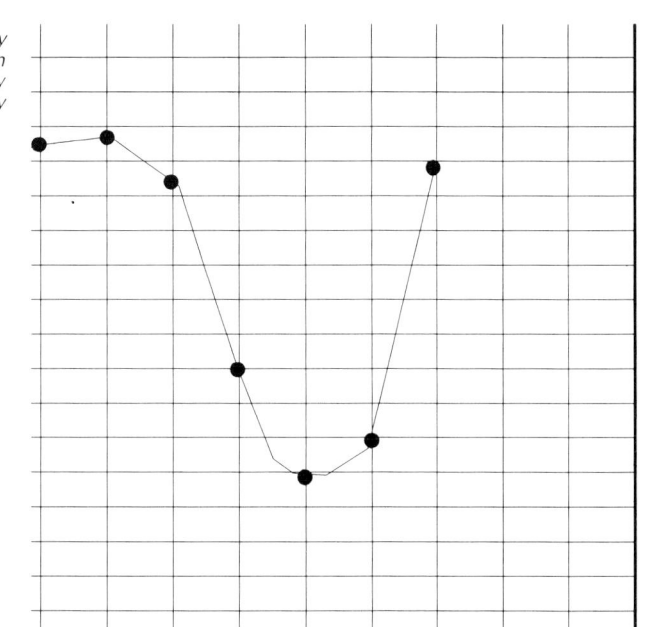

The narrow valley causes you to be much more concerned about adjusting draw length. Care must be taken if you are going to take advantage of the extra speed of the cam and still be somewhat comfortable.

Drawing the **line of maximum leverage** through the cam is a bit more difficult than with the round wheel. We begin at the axle as before, but locating the center of the cam is the tricky part. Most wheels have some type of marking or hole at the geometric center. This point can be used with the axle to determine the line of maximum leverage. If you have difficulty finding the line of maximum leverage, then you must rely on a scale and winch device to make a force-draw curve. Once you have found the middle of the valley then you can draw the line of maximum leverage through the cam.

The pictures provided show the line of maximum leverage of three different cams (Fig. 45a, 45b and 45c) and a sequence of the line of maximum leverage before the cam reaches the valley (Fig. 46), in the valley (Fig. 47), and after the cam passes the valley (Fig. 48). These pictures show that the cam rotates through the same positions as the round wheel.

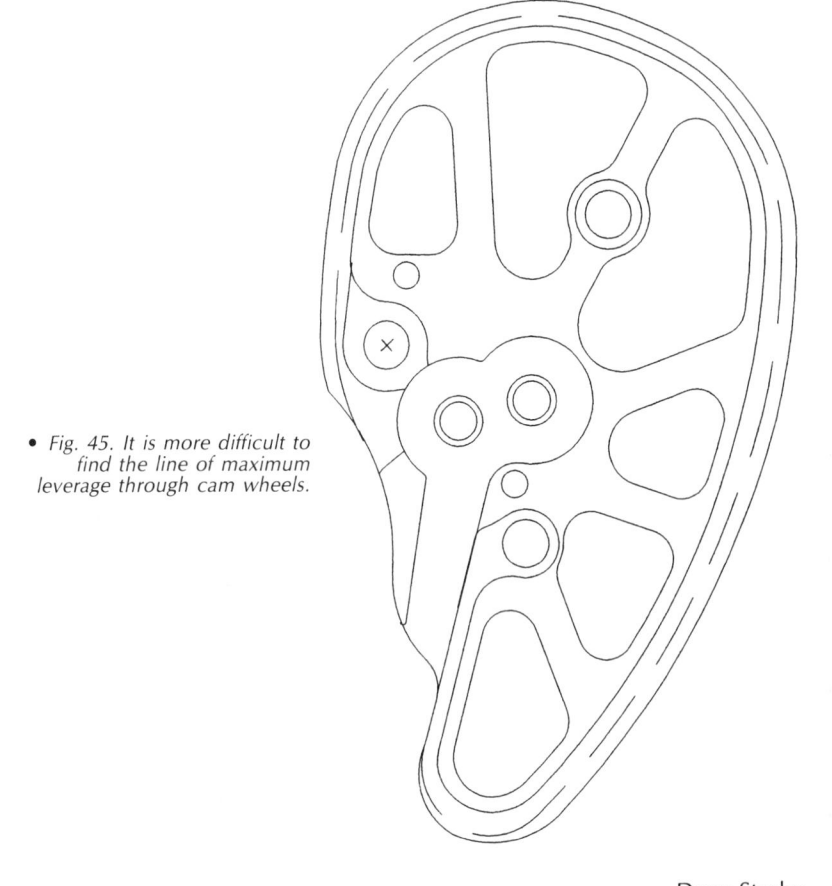

• *Fig. 45. It is more difficult to find the line of maximum leverage through cam wheels.*

Draw Stroke

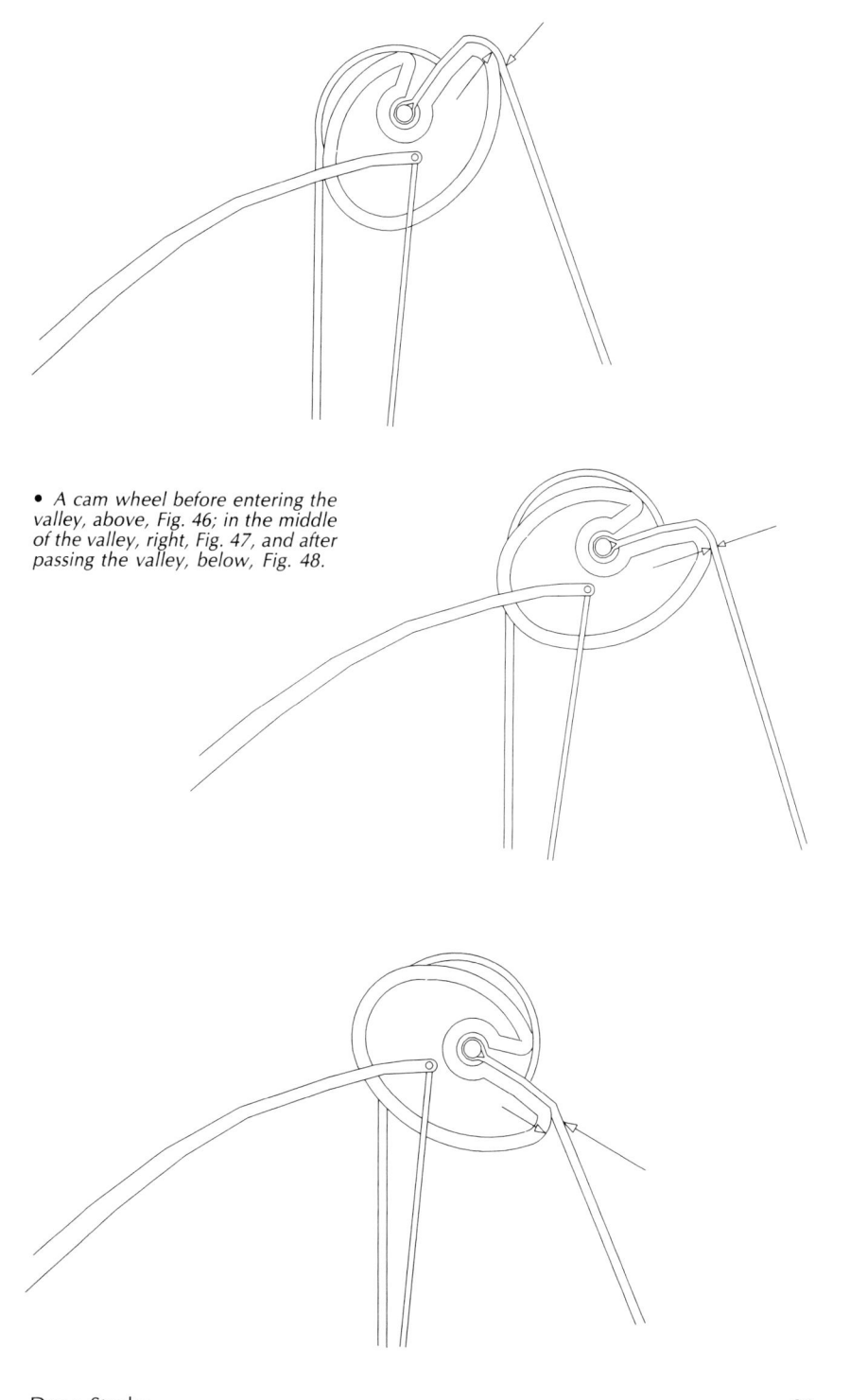

• *A cam wheel before entering the valley, above, Fig. 46; in the middle of the valley, right, Fig. 47, and after passing the valley, below, Fig. 48.*

D: Limb Deflection

While the eccentric wheels are doing their rolling, energy is being stored in the limbs of the bow. Therefore, it is important to note the action of the limbs during this process.

The static deflection of a limb is very closely related to the performance of the bow. Static deflection is the measure of the pre-bend of the limb. The diagram shows the limb being measured while the bow is in the brace position (Fig. 49). The bend is measured from a straight line which extends from the surface on the butt of the limb to the same surface at the end of the limb. **The optimum range for static deflection is usually from two to four inches depending upon limb design.**

If the limbs on your bow are mounted so they have little pre-bend, then good bow performance is hard to achieve. On the bright side, your limbs should last a long time because they will not work hard when the bow is drawn. On the other side of the coin, if the static deflection of your bow limbs is more than four inches then the limbs may be over-stressed when at full draw and will be unstable.

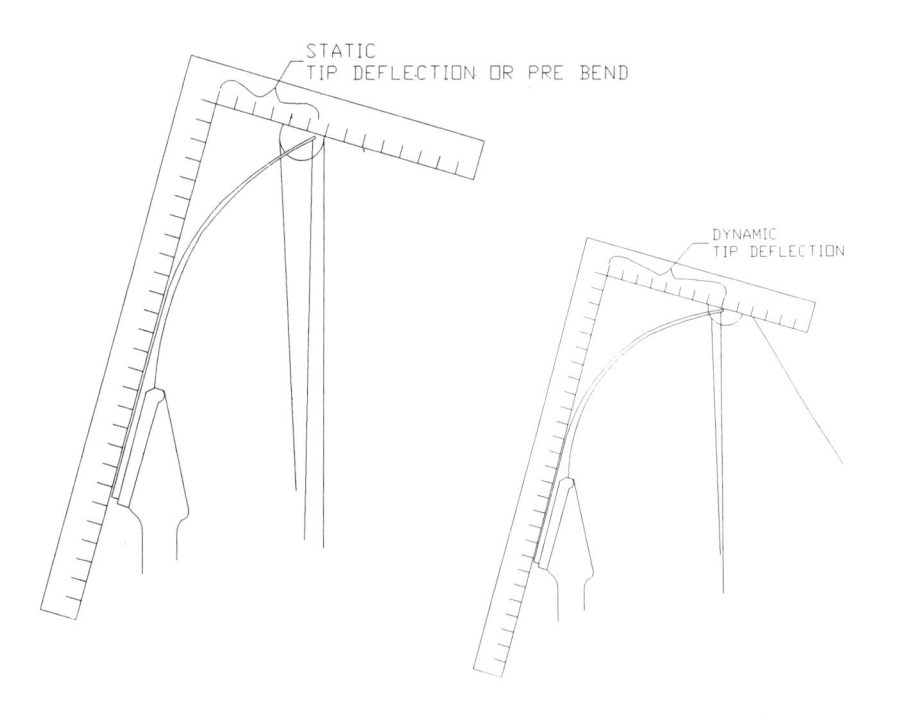

• *Fig. 49. Use a roofing square to measure static tip deflection (pre-bend), left. Fig. 50, above, do the same thing to measure the limb bend at full draw.*

At full draw, this deflection can be called the **dynamic deflection**. The optimum range for dynamic deflection varies with limb design, but on many bows that I have it is from five to seven inches. Bending beyond this range may compress the inner layer of fiberglass beyond the point where it works best. Bending below this range does not allow the limbs to reach their best performance level but may give longer limb life. If you desire **high performance**, you must take advantage of the material in the limbs of your bow; you must make them work, not loaf.

Filament-reinforced plastic limbs have the same basic deflection ranges as the older wood-core limbs but will withstand slightly higher dynamic stresses. It is a good idea to check the factory warranty on these limbs before stressing them beyond six inches at full draw.

E: The Multiple Draw Length Eccentric Wheel

Fitting a new archer or a growing archer with the correct draw length is not an easy task. Dealers had to change wheel sizes and alter string lengths quite often until bow manufacturers started producing the multiple draw length eccentric wheel.

The multiple draw length slots in an eccentric wheel make one wheel provide the force-draw curves of several different sizes of wheels (Fig. 51). Each slot usually provides a **change of about one inch in draw length**. A given tri-draw wheel, for example, could provide the shooter with a valley at 29 inches or 30 inches or 31 inches, depending upon the slot used. The shortest

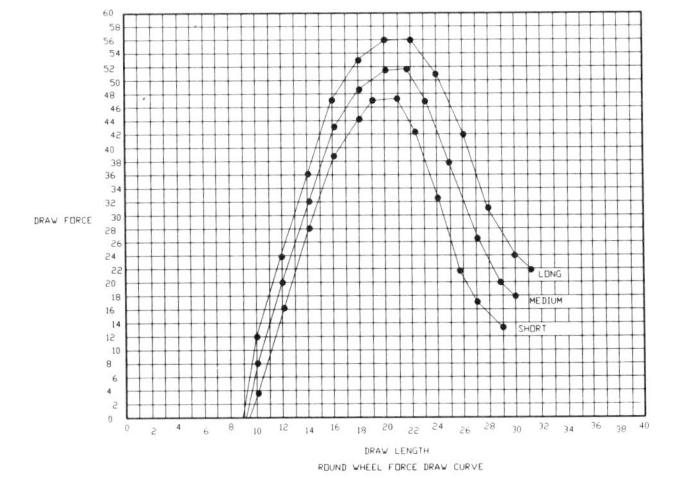

- *Fig. 51. A tri-draw wheel will produce three different draw lengths with three separate force-draw curves.*

draw length on these wheels is obtained by placing the cables in the slots toward the outside of the bow as shown (Fig. 52). The longest draw length is obtained by placing the cables in the slots toward the inside of the bow (Fig. 54). The same bow will give the three force-draw curves in the diagram.

As the draw length is increased by moving the cable to another slot, the limb bend at full draw is also increased. This translates into about five pounds more added peak weight for each inch of draw length added.

The amount of let-off will also increase as draw length is increased. The long draw length of the multiple draw wheel will have about 10 percent more let-off than the short draw length.

Many of the bows with multiple draw length wheels will show their best performance when set in the short or medium draw lengths. The reasons for this are increased pre-bend in the limbs in the shorter draw lengths and the lower let-off. Both of these characteristics make the cable system tighter and more consistent.

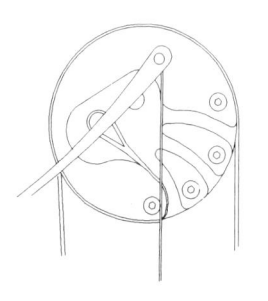 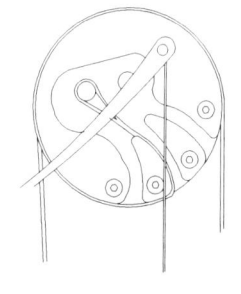 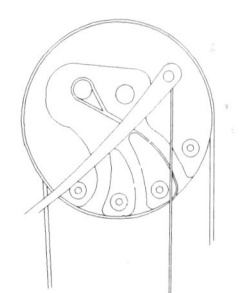

• *Fig. 52, left. The slot toward the outside of the bow produces the shortest draw length of the multiple-draw wheel. Fig. 53, center. Using the middle slot will produce the medium draw length of this wheel. Fig. 54, right. The slot toward the inside of the bow will generate the longest draw length.*

Draw Stroke

Chapter 3B

The Single-Cam Bow

Section 3B-A: The Force-Draw Curve

The force-draw curve created by the single-cam bow is similar in all aspects to other medium energy cam systems. The force required to draw the single-cam bow increases quickly to peak weight, stays there for several inches of the draw stroke and then drops even quicker into a narrow valley. The curve in Fig. 3B.01shows the broad, rounded top of one of my own single-cam test bows which uses a 65% let-off Matthews Pro cam mounted on the bottom limb.

Drawing the single-cam bow also feels just like any other cam bow. In fact, if you were blindfolded you couldn't tell the difference. You would be able to distinguish it from a round wheel by its quick drop into the valley and by its much tighter, solid sound on release.

The stored energy of the bow used in Fig. 3B.01 is 57 foot-pounds. This was calculated using the weight measurements that form the curve: 0 at 9 inches, 8, 14, 21, 26, 30, 35, 39, 41, 44, 45.5, 47, 48, 48.5, 48.5, 47, 44, 37, 31, 22, and 19 at 29 inches.

To measure the efficiency of this single-cam test bow, I shot a 450 grain arrow through the chronograph. Its speed was 258 feet per second, which yields a kinetic energy of 45 foot-pounds. This value compared to a stored energy of 57 foot-pounds computes an

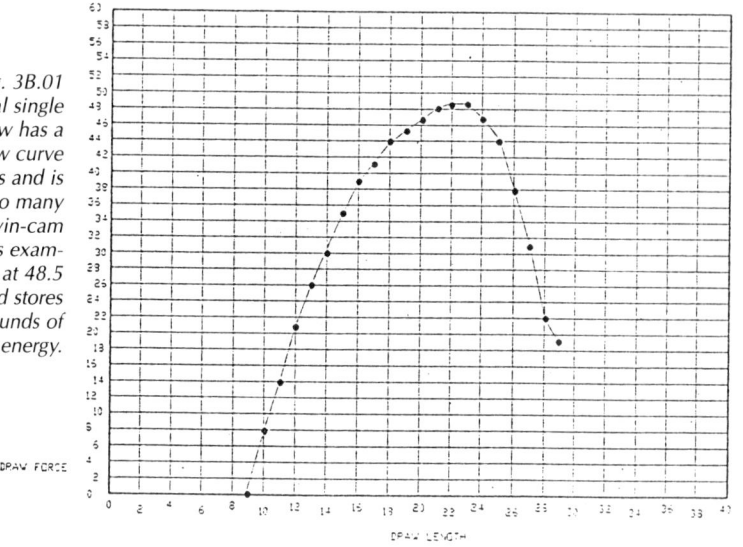

• Fig. 3B.01
A typical single
cam bow has a
force-draw curve
like this and is
similar to many
medium twin-cam
bows. This exam-
ple peaks at 48.5
pounds and stores
57 foot-pounds of
energy.

efficiency of 78.9% , which means this bow is doing a very good job of transferring its energy to the arrow.

The single-cam bows, on average, are yielding AMO standard (540 grains, 30 inch draw and 60 pounds draw weight) arrow velocities of 230 to 235 feet per second. That's real good velocity but not as high as some of the more radically designed two-cam bows which test at velocities in excess of 245 and 250 fps. The biggest reason for the faster velocities from these two-cam bows is their ability to store more energy at the beginning of the draw stroke, as you will see later in the chapter on super-cams.

A single-cam by Matthews with a weighted nose is generating as much arrow velocity as any twin-super cam and is competing for its slice of the market. The weight increases the momentum of the wheel and transfers more energy to the arrow at the end of the power stroke but tunes the same as the regular single-cam.

Section 3B-B: How The Single-Cam Works

The main purpose and advantage of the single-cam bow is to avoid the timing adjustment which all two-cam bows require. To do this, a single cam-shaped, three-track wheel, with axle off center, is designed for and mounted on the lower limb of a traditionally styled compound bow (Fig. 3B.02). It could just as easily have been placed

• Fig. 3B.02 (far right)
Most single cams are mounted
on the lower limb with a round
idler pulley mounted on top.

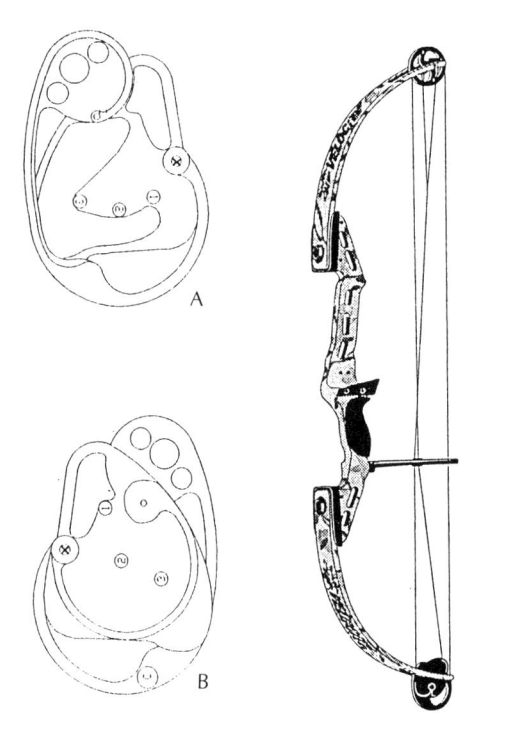

• Fig. 3B.03 (A, B, C)
Drawing A shows
the major string
track of a typical
single cam with the
axle located at the
X. Drawing B shows
the minor string
track, while C
shows the end view
with the center
cable track between
the two string tracks.

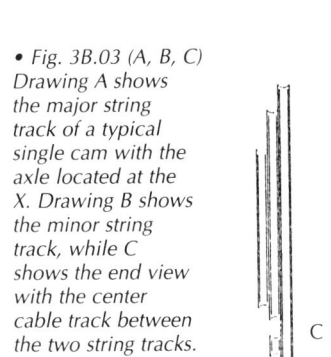

on the top limb, but the bottom seems to be the preference due to the travel path considerations given to the nocking point of the string.

Opposite the single cam on the top limb is a true pulley or idler wheel. This center-axle, single-track wheel has a simple purpose: to bend the top limb approximately the same amount as the bottom limb. Both limbs will then store nearly equal amounts of energy and supply nearly equal amounts of thrust to the arrow. Nearly equal amounts of thrust make the bow more consistent and easier to tune.

The resulting design does not require any synchronization between wheels since the top wheel is only a simple center-mounted pulley and has no affect on the shape of the force-draw curve of the bow. Changing either string or cable length results only in a draw length change, due to a cam rotation change of a few degrees in either direction. **The simple rules of string length remain the same: a shorter string makes shorter draw length, while a shorter cable makes longer draw length.**

The single cam has two string tracks on the outer edges of the wheel with a cable track between them (Fig. 3B.03). The string

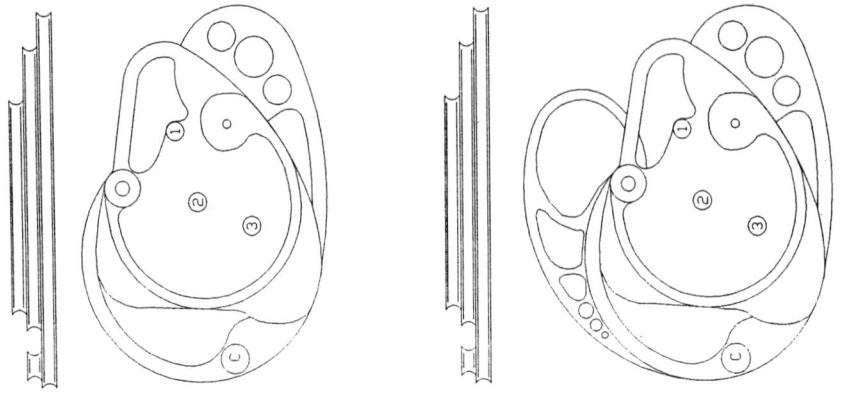

• *Fig. 3B.04. The cam on the left allows the string to exit the wheel close to the axle, while the cam on the right has added radius to keep the string the same distance from the axle as it is on the top idler wheel.*

tracks are of different shape and diameter but both reel out string as the bow is drawn, just like on a standard two-wheel compound. The major string track, for right handers, is on the left side of the wheel as you look down while drawing the bow, and the smaller, minor string track is on the right.

The minor track reels out less string; the string rolls outward over the idler wheel toward the archer and causes the top limb to bend. This action also affects the travel path of the nocking point on the string. The most desirable path for the nock during the power stroke is level and every effort is made to create this by controlling the relative sizes of the two string tracks as they relate to the center track.

Most of the single-cams I've seen have several anchor pins (see Fig. 3B.03) for each end of the string, allowing you to make minor adjustments to draw length. Each time you change the string anchor on either end or on both ends, you must reset the nocking point to its original height since both ends are not necessarily affected equally.

When you pull more string into the center of the wheel, the amount between the two wheels is lessened, making a shorter draw length. If string is let out of the wheel, the draw length is increased. With either adjustment, the draw weight changes in the same direction as the draw length change in about the same **five-pounds-per-inch** ratio as standard compounds.

The center cable track reels in cable and controls when the force-draw reaches its peak, how long it stays there and when it drops into the valley. By holding the bow at peak over a longer distance the draw length can be increased, but each draw length requires a different size wheel. This points out the major disadvantage of the single-cam bow -- to make a major change in draw length you must purchase a different wheel size.

The tiller measurements of the top and bottom limbs may be different on the single cam bow due to the design of the cam. If the major string track is such that the string exits the cam while being very close to the axle (within 1/2 inch) then the lower limb tiller will be less than the top limb (Fig. 3B.04). This is because the top idler wheel, with its axle in the center, keeps the string about one and a half inches from the axle. The more recently designed cams have added radius at the string exit point so that it is the same distance from the cam axle as the idler axle. This feature aids in creating a level nock path during the power stroke while creating equal tiller measurements.

A simple method for measuring and setting tiller on the single- cam bow is to connect a string line to both axles. Using this instead of the bowstring as a reference, set the tiller measurements equal or at whatever setting you prefer. To check the tiller just reattach the string line to the axles and measure.

So, without having to put two cams into a synchronized rotation, you can have the energy and speed of a compound cam bow with only one cam. Eccentric wheel timing is not an issue with this bow as long as the string runs freely over the idler wheel. If you elect to terminate the string at the top idler, the whole ball game changes and timing becomes a big issue again. That's because changing the length of one part of the string will rotate the cam one way or the other.

Section 3B-C: Tuning Your Single-Cam Bow

Tuning the single-cam bow is greatly simplified compared to tuning the two-cam type, because you don't have to spend time getting the cams synchronized. Beyond that, the same tuning steps are used for all types of compounds since they all cast an arrow through the bow handle and over an arrow rest. They all create arrow flight, and that will always need adjusting.

As with any compound bow that is draw length adjustable, the top priority in tuning is setting draw length correctly. The bow has to feel comfortable before you can perform at your best. Liken it to selecting a pair of hunting boots that fit well.

MAJOR ADJUSTMENTS: Depending upon the design, each single-cam wheel size is adjustable across one and a half inches of draw length. Therefore, the first step is getting the right size cam for you. If you're new in archery, find a good dealer to help with selection so that if you don't get the right size on the first try, he's there to help correct the situation.

If you have a chance to look at several different single-cam draw length sizes, you'll notice a difference in the center tract design. The longer draw cams will have a longer center tract to hold the draw force at peak over a longer distance before letting it drop into the valley. It's best if you can get the wheel size that puts you in the middle of its draw adjustment range so you have the capability of adjusting the draw longer or shorter as needed.

Once you have the correct size, search through the various draw length adjustments to get the best fit. Again, if you're new in archery, a dealer or knowledgeable friend can help you make the right adjustments.

A look at a typical single-cam also will help. In Fig. 3B.03a you can see the string anchor pins on the major string side, while Fig. 3B.03b shows the pins on the minor side of the same cam. These pins anchor the ends of the bow string and determine the length of string between the top and bottom limbs, which determines the draw length.

Pin 3 on either side will yield the shortest draw length for this wheel. Moving one string end only to Pin 2 will increase draw length about 1/8 to 1/4 inch, depending upon how far apart the pins are. Move the other string end to Pin 2 and you'll get another 1/8 to 1/4 inch. Do the same with Pin 3 and you'll get more draw length. Over all, you can make adjustments totaling 1 1/2 inches. One of these settings will be the best for you.

MINOR ADJUSTMENTS: There are two ways to get optimum draw length with minor adjustments on a single-cam bow—the same two ways as for standard two-cam bows. One is to twist the string, and the other is to twist the power cable. Either affects draw on a small scale and helps to fine tune draw length to its best setting for you.

As with any bow, I add about 15 to 20 twists to the string when I install it. Then when I need to make a fine adjustment to the draw, I can either add or subtract twists to make it right. Adding three or four twists to the string makes the draw length about 1/16 inch shorter.

I do the same to the single power cable of my single-cam bows. Adding twists to the cable, however, will increase draw length since the cam is being back-rolled by the shorter cable. Since there is only one cable to work with, many shooters I know work only with cable twists to adjust draw length. In fact, most start with the draw a little short, add three or four twists and retest for comfort. If you want to try this, continue the twisting and testing until you feel the draw has passed the comfort stage and gotten too long, then reset it shorter. Because we change when shooting a new bow, I recommend you do this periodically to be sure the draw length is still set the best for you. One thing I will warn you about is peep rotation. When I had no twists in my one-cam string the peep came back fairly consistently. When I had a few twists in the string, the peep was not consistent at all. With twenty or more twists the peep got very consistent again, just as with my other bows.

NOCKING POINT LOCATION: Many of the archers I know who are shooting the single-cam are using a nocking point that is a little higher than that needed on a two-cam bow. A height of 3/8 to 5/8 inches above the level of the rest seems to be what is working well for the current design of the single cam. Because of this difference, you should experiment with different settings in this range to find what works best for your bow and arrow combination. Paper testing may show you what is best but shoot testing is still going to be the proof of the pudding.

NOCK FIT: As always, check the fit of the nock on the bowstring. If it is too tight, your arrows may slam into the side of the rest and appear to act stiff. If it is too loose, it may slide down the string when the string is released, causing a high arrow. Nocks should snap onto the string but not slide up and down unless pulled or pushed with a little force. If they snap on but slide loosely, add two strands to the bowstring or increase the size of the center serving. Remember, if you change nock styles you may have to retune, because the fit is different.

STRING AND CABLE MATERIALS: With so many different materials available today, it's hard to figure out what you should use on your own bow when your originals break. Most manufacturers are using a blend of Dyneema and no-stretch Vectran which works well on high tension cam bows. Some manufacturers are using the Dyneema products like the BCY Dynaflight 97 for the cables and the blended no-stretch materials on the string. I recommend that you follow your bow manufacturer's guidelines on these materials. If you want to experiment, check to be sure you won't void the warranty by using any particular material.

I've used them all, in all combinations, and have had no problems with any of them. I've even used dacron for the string, with the others for cables. They sound different but all seem to perform well in the accuracy department. The dacron is the slowest; the Dyneema products wear the best, and the Vectran blends are the fastest.

One problem I have with my single-cam bow is making the

string for it. It is 100 inches long and needs two center servings, one for the nocking point and another for running over the idler wheel. Not only that, my string jig is only 70 inches long.

A friend, Joe Cox from Wisconsin, has invented what he calls the "missing link". It solves this string-making problem (Fig.3B.05). This 3/4 inch long, double ended teardrop link allows you to build two fifty inch strings and hook them together to make the 100 inch string for your single-cam bow. Not only that, the end serving of one string conveniently runs over the idler wheel. Further, you don't need a new string jig.

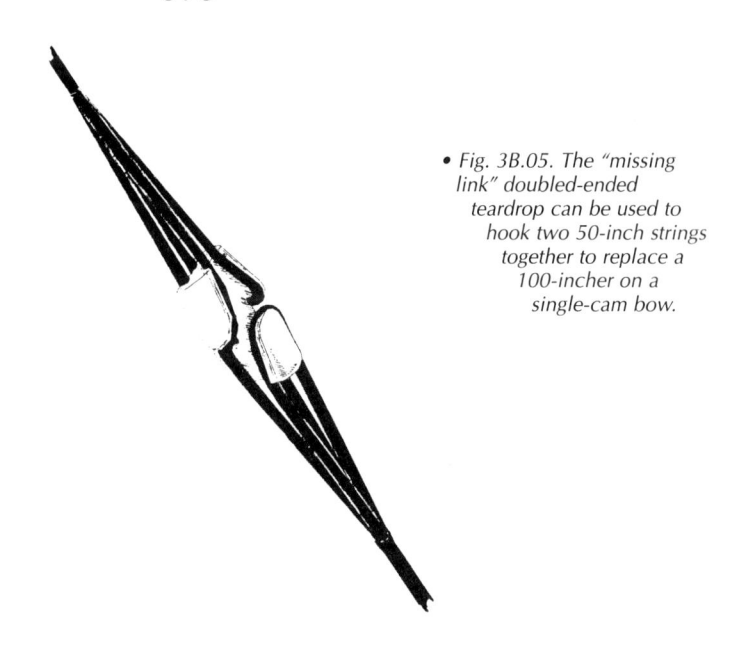

• Fig. 3B.05. The "missing link" doubled-ended teardrop can be used to hook two 50-inch strings together to replace a 100-incher on a single-cam bow.

As the illustration shows, I use a double loop on the string ends that hook to the link. Single loops will do, but I liked the balanced look so I made them double. With this hook up I can experiment with new strings on the nocking side without having to replace the back half. That way, if the nock doesn't fit properly I can make a new front half and get the fit I need. It's a great practical invention. I recommend using it if you make your own strings or know someone who does.

FINAL TUNING STEPS: The remaining tuning steps for the single cam bow are the same as standard two-cam bows. Just follow the information and procedures outlined earlier in this book and you will have success tuning your single-cam compound bow.

Chapter 3C

The Super-Cam Bow

Section 3C-A: The Force-Draw Curve

"Speed is everything" some people think. In fact, so many archers feel that way they are driving the archery industry toward the maximum speed attainable from a hand held bow. How do I know this? By comparing the force-draw curve of the super cams being made now to the maximum practical force-draw curve.

The maximum practical curve looks like Fig. 3C.01, where the draw weight goes straight up as the string is first drawn and stays at peak weight during the entire draw stroke until it drops into the valley during the last inch. This curve creates the most area between it and the horizontal axis. In other words, this curve has the most stored energy possible under practical circumstances. The only way to get more energy stored is to avoid dropping the weight into the valley and that's not practical. (At least, not to me it isn't.)

Today's super-cams come close to the maximum energy curve by creating a force-draw curve like the one in Fig. 3C.02. In this curve, the weight does not go straight up at the beginning of the draw stroke, but it does go up fast, which requires a great amount of energy to be supplied by the archer. The drop into the valley by most super cams takes place over only two to three inches, making lots of area between the curve and the horizontal axis below.

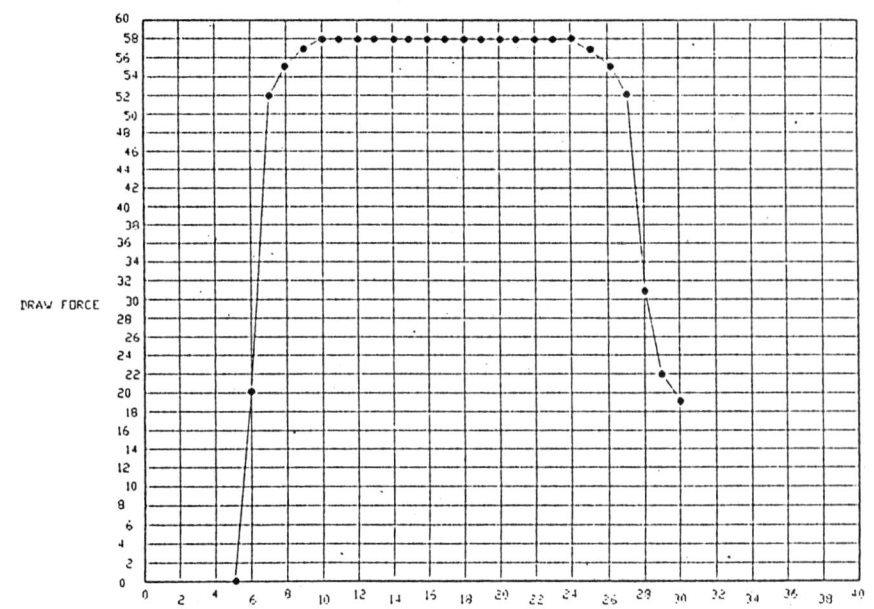

FORCE DRAW CURVE

• Fig. 3C.01. A bow which stores the most possible energy would have a force-draw curve that goes almost straight up at the beginning, stays at peak for the entire draw stroke and drops to the valley in the last inch. Today's bows are approaching this level of stored energy.

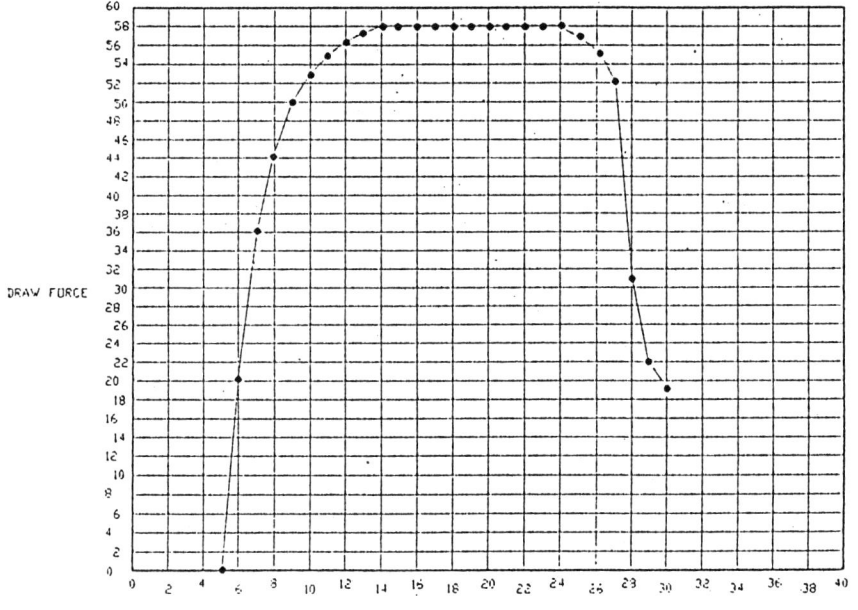

FORCE DRAW CURVE

• *Fig. 3C.02. This twin-cam bow peaks at 60 pounds and stores 95.6 foot-pounds of energy. This high stored energy is partly due to the low brace height of five inches.*

The stored energy calculation for this bow is as follows:

S.E. = 12+28+37+45+53+57+59+59+60+60+60+60+60
      +60+60+60+60+60+59+58+54+42+32+12

S.E. = 1148 inch-pounds

Divide inch-pounds by 12 to find foot-pounds and **S.E. = 95.6 ft-lbs.** This is a very high amount of stored energy for 60 pounds of peak draw weight and is getting close to the most stored energy possible using a hand held bow.

The next question is, how much of this stored energy does a bow like this give to the arrow? If it's not very efficient, then you've spent a lot of energy for little gain. If it's 75 % efficient or better, then you're going to get a very fast arrow from the 95.6 ft-lbs. stored by this bow.

If this bow shoots a 400 grain arrow at 280 feet per second, the arrow will have 69.7 foot-pounds of energy. The arrow's energy of 69.7 foot-pounds divided by the stored energy of 95.6 foot-pounds yields an efficiency of 73 %. That's good efficiency for a big cam.

As is the case with most bows, the heavier arrow will receive a higher percent of the stored energy than will a light arrow. The difference is substantial, but the light arrow still flies at a great enough velocity to attract many 3-D archery enthusiasts and bowhunters.

The trademark of the big cam is the sharp dropoff into the valley. To many it's unnerving to have such a drop in weight over such a short distance but necessary to get the arrow velocity. The price you pay for the speed is in the time you spend tuning these big cams, which is usually more than for medium cams or energy wheel cams.

Another price is paid in comfort. Just when you reach the point in the draw stroke where your shoulder is losing it's leverage, you have to keep drawing peak weight several more inches. The added stress takes its toll and can stop your archery game in its tracks unless you take proper care of your body. Warming up shoulder and back muscles before shooting should be part of your normal routine, just like stretching after shooting.

Section 3C-B: Handle Design

To get more speed from super cam bows, manufacturers have designed the handles with lower brace heights. (See Fig. 3C.03) The direct result of this reflex design is a longer power stroke, since the arrow is nocked on the string over a longer distance. The longer the power stroke, the more energy gets transferred to the arrow.

A straight handle design has a brace height of about nine

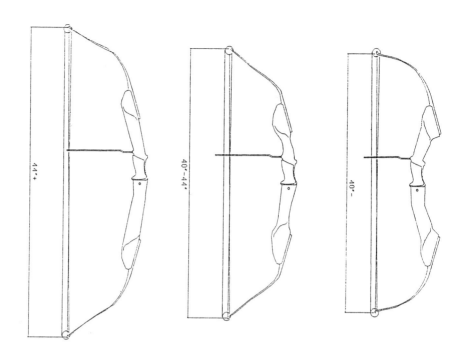

• Fig. 3C.03. The handle on the left is a short reflex design which has a low brace height and is designed to yield more speed. The longer handles are straight and deflex, which aid in aiming stability but are slower.

inches. When 30 inches of arrow have been drawn behind the arrow rest and released, energy is transferred to the arrow over 21 inches (30 - 9). With a reflex handle and limbs mounted at an almost vertical angle, brace heights of five to six inches can be achieved. This increases the power stroke to 24 or 25 inches, and in most bows each inch of power stroke adds about seven to ten feet per second to the arrow velocity. That's how super-cam bows achieve AMO speeds of 250 fps and faster.

You must always keep in mind that the velocity of the arrow depends on more than the ability of the bow to store energy. As mentioned earlier, the bow must operate efficiently when delivering that energy to the arrow. So when you see the big cams on a bow, check it's low brace height.

Be aware, also, that you need to look closer. You need to look at axle and bearing material and design. Check limb and handle material and bearing material and design. Check limb and handle material. Does the cable harness have a lot of parts which might lower the efficiency and slow the arrow?

Here's a big item for hunters: will the bow be noisy or too hard to draw slowly, with minimal movement, i.e., just your drawing arm? Your purpose of use has to be kept in mind regardless of the arrow velocity you might get, because comfort is conducive to consistent performance.

Section 3C-C: Tuning The Big Cams

DRAW LENGTH: Some extra considerations must be given to the super-cam bow when tuning it for accuracy. The first of these is how you will adjust the draw length to get it to fit you properly. The easiest major draw length adjustment method uses modules, while changing wheel sizes is the more difficult.

Most super-cams have a draw length adjustment range of six inches, from 26 to 31 inches. Each inch has its own module which is attached to the cable side of the cam wheel with two or three screws. In most cases the module can be removed without putting the bow in a press. This makes the job easy for anyone.

If you have a short draw length of 28 or fewer inches, remember that you will not achieve the high velocities advertised for a given bow. Each inch of draw stroke translates to seven to ten feet per second in arrow velocity, so shorter draw means less velocity. I caution you not to exaggerate your draw length by anchoring behind your ear. Bad form cannot be overcome by the added arrow velocity you might get. A fast miss is still a miss!

As with any other compound bow, the finer adjustments to draw length can be made using string anchor pins, twisting the string or twisting the cables. The same rule applies here: **more string between the wheels makes more draw length, while more cable makes less draw length.**

WHEEL TIMING: Getting the two cams to work together is critical to achieving accuracy with the super-cam bow. One twist on one cable can make a big difference in arrow grouping. That's why you must spend time finding that specific timing setting which makes your bow shoot the best.

As mentioned elsewhere in this book, wheel timing or rollover is controlled by the relative cable lengths. If both cables are the same length, then both wheels roll over the same, and tuning the arrow rest and nocking point will produce good arrow flight and grouping consistency. The mistake most archers make here is to have a preconceived notion as to what the cams should look like when they are in time. I suggest that you let the bow tell you when they are in time by working through the cable tuning procedure outlined in another chapter until you get the best arrow groups. You have to do this because of variables like slightly unmatched limbs, hand position, cable and string material, etc.

NOCKING POINT: Super-cam bows are usually short, which places extra pinch on the nock when the bow is drawn. That's why many archers use a rope loop tied on the bowstring above and below the nock to relieve most of the pinch. This loop allows the bowstring to run through the nock throat at right angles to the nock all through the draw and power stroke. Most shooters feel that cleaner arrow flight is attainable with the loop.

See the example and instructions on page 102.

Even with the loop, the nocking point has to be adjusted up and down the string to find where the best arrow flight and arrow groups can be achieved. As before, shoot test different nocking point settings from 40 or 50 yards if you feel comfortable shooting that far from the target.

The super-cam demands that you be persistent when tuning. With a little work, it will shoot accurately and fast. That, along with practice, will get the results you want.

• On the bigger big game, especially at shorter distances, speed is not as important as arrow penetration and kinetic energy. A heavier, slower arrow will also be part of a quieter shooting unit. The carbon arrow gets deep penetration from its small diameter and lower amount of bending on impact; its energy stays in line better.

Super-Cam Bow

Chapter 4
Shooting From The Valley

What you read in this chapter is absolutely the **most important part of tuning the compound bow.** If you don't plan on adjusting your bow so you shoot it from the middle of the valley, then don't plan on winning the tournament next week and don't plan on taking that trophy whitetail next hunting season. In fact, don't plan on your bow working in your favor in any moment of crisis. The compound bow is a great shooting machine but only if you make it work the way it was designed and built to work — from the **middle of the valley.**

Good arrow response is the final objective of every archer, and with some basic knowledge of the force-draw curve and arrow response as the bow is released from different positions in and near the valley, good arrow performance can be achieved. The area in front of the valley is defined as the front slope, the area behind the valley is defined as the wall, and of course there is the valley. As the bow is drawn to and released from each of these areas in the force-draw curve, any given arrow will respond differently. These responses are the subject of this chapter.

Further, by shooting from the middle of the valley, you can **fine tune your bow to a specific arrow shaft.** Changing shaft sizes every time your bow doesn't group well is rather expensive. Although changing shaft sizes is sometimes necessary, it is far easier to make adjustments to current equipment and utilize shafts you already own. These adjustments are what is called fine tuning, and fine tuning begins in the middle of the valley.

A: Arrow Response From The Front Slope
The front slope of the force-draw curve is that section of the curve which is between the peak and the valley (Fig. 55). During the draw cycle the front slope represents the let-off of the weight felt on the string. The slope is showing a decrease in weight during the draw cycle as the bow string is drawn.

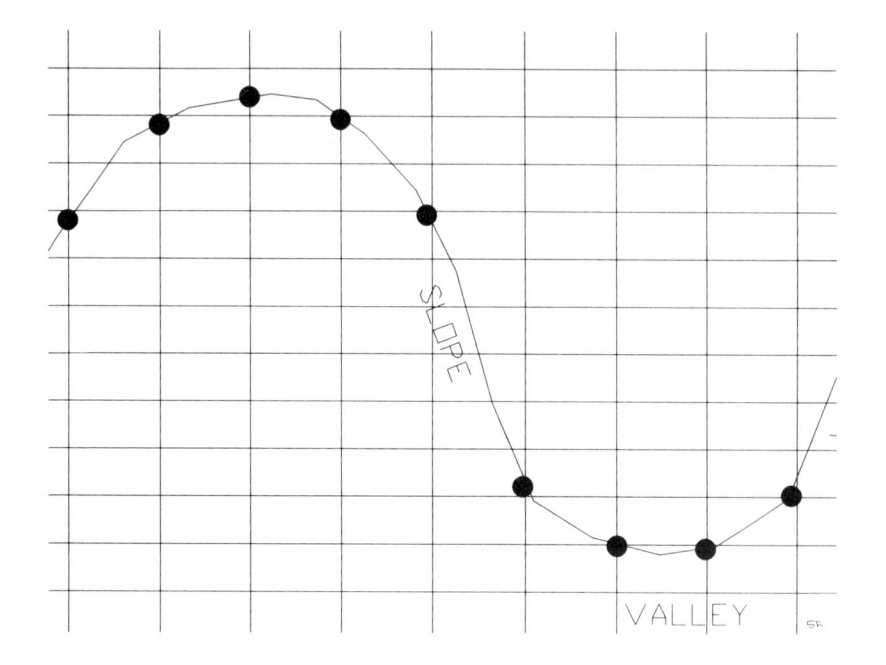

• *Fig. 55. The front slope is between the peak and valley and shows rapidly decreasing weight.*

When the bow string is released, the slope takes on the opposite roll and shows that the weight on the string is increasing toward peak weight. This increase in weight provides an accelerated start for the arrow.

Should you be anchored on this slope and release your arrow from that position, then the arrow will be given a harsh, suddenly-accelerated start. This jam start can cause an arrow to shoot erratically high. Please note that this is **opposite** to the reaction you would get from a recurve bow which was shot from an underdrawn position. With the compound, underdrawing or shooting from the slope starts the arrow at a higher weight than if the arrow had been shot from the valley.

A second condition resulting from shooting from the front slope is the high probability that no two shots can be started at the same weight. Because the draw weight is changing so rapidly on the slope, and because few archers can anchor exactly the same for any two shots, the weight at which each arrow is started can vary greatly. A one-eighth inch change in draw length can mean a one- to two-pound change in draw weight if you are not anchored in the valley.

Arrows perform inconsistently when shot from the front slope, and so do you when you release from there. **Creeping** forward at the time of release is a **common problem** of those shooting from the front slope. The best example of this problem occurs when the bowhunter is in a tree stand. Most archers have a tendency to underdraw when shooting uphill and downhill. So the bowhunter who underdraws, while shooting from a tree stand, may overshoot his target and think it was because he misjudged the distance when he actually got an erratic high arrow because the arrow was released from the front slope.

B: Arrow Response From The Wall

The wall, or the "stops" as it is sometimes called, is that part of the force-draw curve which occurs after the valley (Fig. 56). The reason it is called the "stops" by some people is that when the bow is drawn beyond the middle of the valley the draw weight increases so abruptly that the increase in weight stops the draw process. Simply put, you reach the limit of your strength and cannot draw the bow any further. This section of the force-draw curve is the steepest part and appears to be almost vertical on the chart.

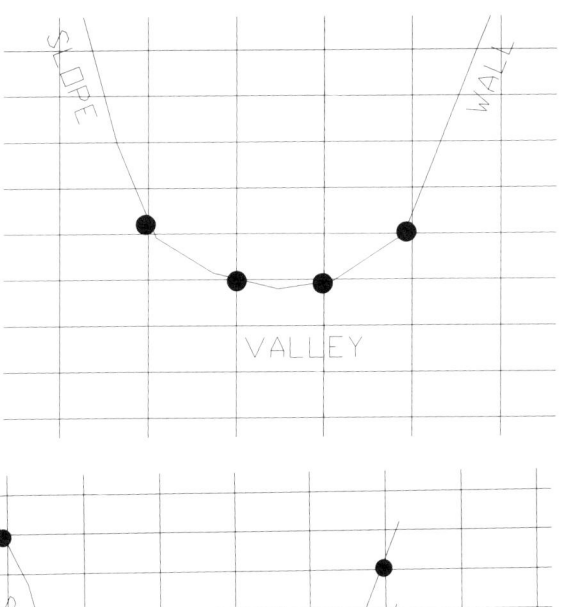

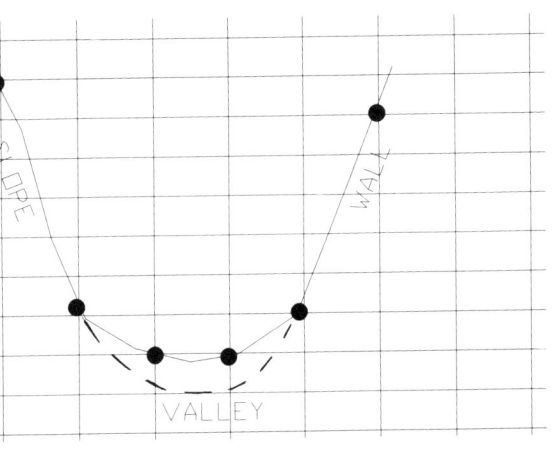

• Fig. 56, top. The wall is the near-vertical portion of the curve which occurs when drawing beyond the valley. Fig. 57, bottom. When the compound bow is released from behind the valley, the weight on the string drops below the valley weight.

Response of arrows shot from the wall is even **more erratic** than arrows shot from the slope. Because the draw weight is changing so fast on the wall, any variation in your anchor point will result in a change in holding weight and therefore in the starting weight of a given arrow. Again, it is unlikely that any two arrows will be released with the same starting weight.

The **second disadvantage of shooting on the wall** is the condition of **"weight drop"** when the compound is released. Just as the weight increases after reaching the middle of the valley during the draw cycle, it must retrace its path and decrease during the power stroke. The weight will drop into the valley after the string is released, but this drop in weight is exaggerated. The result is a drop in weight which falls below the weight of the valley (Fig. 57), and in some bows with low efficiency, this drop can be in excess of 10 pounds.

After dropping to a low weight, the string propels the arrow up the front slope of the force-draw curve. This sharp and inconsistent increase in weight is reflected in the response of the arrow. Arrows are given a "ripple start" during this period of sharp decrease and increase in weight. Some arrows will reach the target high while others, for seemingly no reason, will hit the target low. **Broadhead flight is a real disaster when you are anchoring and releasing from the wall.**

At this point we must look at the cam and its force-draw curve to find its weaknesses (Fig. 58). Without much inspection, you should see that the same problems are going to occur with the cam that occur with round eccentric wheels. The only difference is that the **cam exaggerates these problems** because of steeper slopes in front of and behind the valley.

• *Fig. 58. The valley of a cam bow is usually very narrow, with steep slopes in front and behind.*

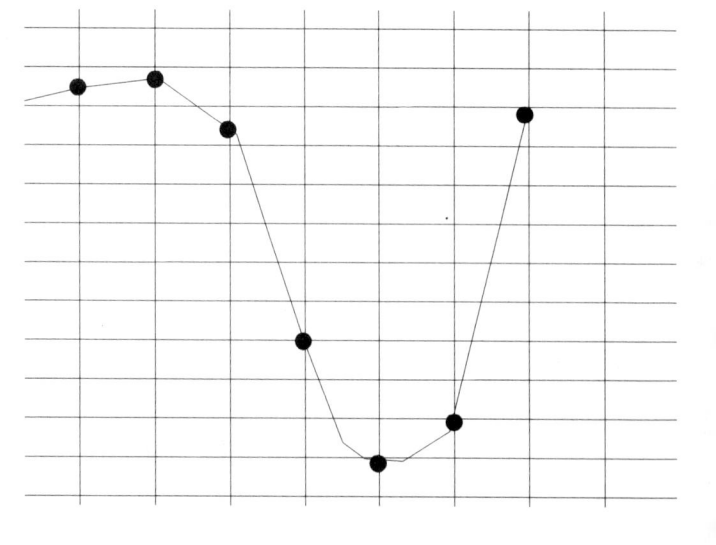

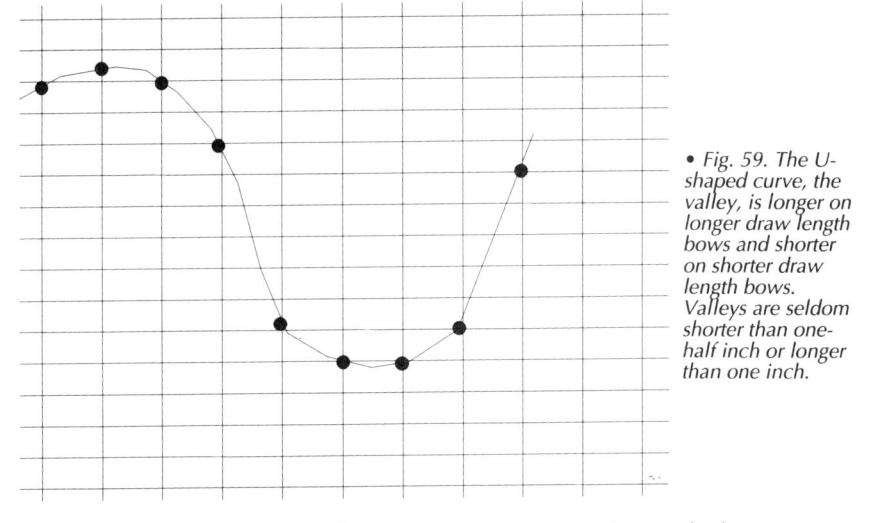

• Fig. 59. The U-shaped curve, the valley, is longer on longer draw length bows and shorter on shorter draw length bows. Valleys are seldom shorter than one-half inch or longer than one inch.

The cam also offers less valley. More precision must be used when measuring the draw length of the bow so as to avoid shooting from the slope or the wall. Because you spend more time tuning the cam bow **you pay a price for the extra speed which is usually achieved.** The ultimate price you pay is in the higher level of consistency with which your body must perform in order to obtain good performance from a short valley and a steep front slope.

C: Arrow Response From The Valley

The force-draw curve of the compound bow is simple to read. Following the curve up to peak and then downward leads the eye to a soft "u" shaped section of curve called the valley (Fig. 59). This valley is of substantial length. **On the longer draw length bows the valley can be as long as one inch. Shorter draw bows have shorter valleys, but most are not shorter than one-half inch.**

The softness of the valley shows that the draw weight is not changing during this section of the draw cycle. Your conclusion must be that **if the bow is shot from any point within this valley, every arrow will receive the same weight thrust when the bow string is released.** Further, the acceleration out of the valley is smooth and gradual.

The round eccentric wheel offers the best possible starting conditions for an arrow shot by a human. The wide valley and the smooth start helps to compensate for some of the inconsistencies of the shooter. And believe me, we all have our moments of inconsistency. Anchoring at different places will not cause any side effects in a bow being shot from the valley. But the **most important feature of the valley is the smoothness of acceleration obtained when releasing an arrow from the valley.**

At this point it should be repeated that the cam has a smaller valley, and the exit from that valley is steeper. For this reason, the cam compensates for fewer of the archer's inconsistencies. That is the price paid for more speed.

D: Draw Length Adjustment Methods

You should have a number of reasons to be shooting from the middle of the valley after reading the previous section. The basic problem that must be dealt with now is how to adjust the draw length of the bow if it is not correct.

Check the two diagrams to remind yourself of your draw situation. Figure 60 shows the eccentric wheels in the position where the draw length of the bow is too short for the shooter. Figure 61 shows the wheels when the draw length is too long for the shooter.

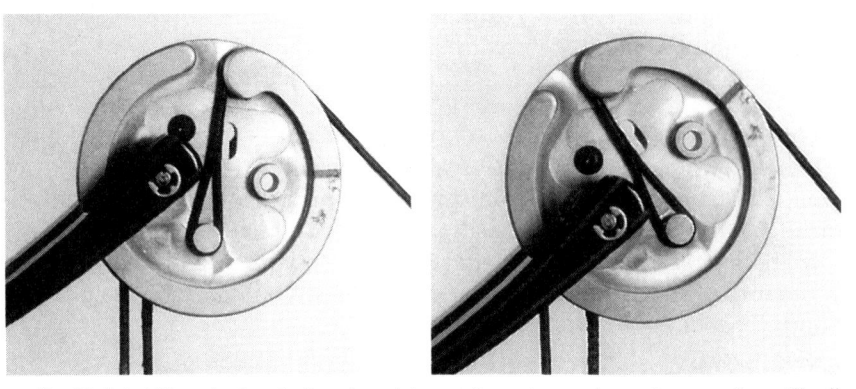

• *Fig. 60, left. When the bow's draw length is too short, the maximum leverage line will roll past the point where the cable leaves the wheel. Fig. 61, right, when the draw length is too long the maximum leverage line will not roll to the point where the cable leaves the wheel.*

Adjusting the draw length for these two conditions requires opposite changes in the wheel/cable system. **To INCREASE the draw length of the bow you must increase the length of cable around the wheel** and to **DECREASE the draw length of the bow you must decrease the length of cable around the wheel.**

To decrease the length of cable around the eccentric wheel, which decreases the draw length of the bow, you can do one of several things. The simplest and cheapest method is to buy a shorter string. If the string is one inch shorter, then one-half inch of string will be taken away from each wheel. The result will be that one-half inch less cable will be wrapped around each wheel. This will cause about three times that much decrease in the draw length of the bow.

You may want to recall some basic math of the circle, which states that the circumference of a circle is slightly larger than three (3.14) times the diameter of the circle. This formula applies to the eccentric wheel any time you change the amount of cable wrapped around the wheel.

The example of one inch is a little on the extreme side, but it serves the purpose. Actually, if you need to make a change that large you should be changing to another wheel size. A one-eighth-inch change in wheel diameter will provide about a one-inch change in draw length.

An alternate way of shortening the draw length of the bow is to change the cable extension on each wheel. The cable extension is the length of cable which extends from the wheel to the string anchor (Fig. 62). Since this cable is attached to the string, shortening the cable extension gives the same result as shortening the string. Change both top and bottom extensions the same amount and be sure that when you are done both extensions are the same length. These extensions are set at the factory when the bow is built and should not have changed unless the cable has slipped.

Again, shortening the cable extension one-eighth inch will shorten the draw length by three-eighths of an inch. If you have to shorten the draw length of the bow by more than one inch, then get the next size smaller wheel.

To lengthen the draw of the bow, you must increase the length of the string or increase the cable extension. The increase of one-eighth inch will cause an increase of three-eighths inch in the draw length. If you need to change draw length more than one inch, then get the next size bigger wheel. Don't forget to change both cable extensions the same amount.

A **problem can be created** when increasing the draw length of any bow by the above methods. If too much cable is allowed to be wrapped around the wheel, then cable overlap may occur (Fig. 63). This means that cable is wrapped completely around the eccentric wheel and is overlapping itself

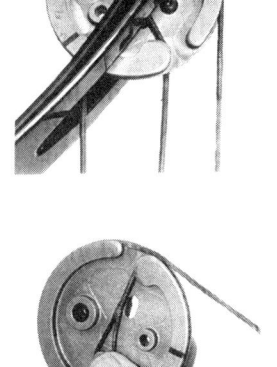

• *Fig. 62, left. Cable extensions act as part of the string and both extensions should be the same length. Fig. 63, above. Cable overlap occurs when too much cable is wrapped around the wheel and will cause poor performance and cable wear.*

as in the picture. The effect of this overlap on arrow performance is very noticeable. Cable wear and damage may result if the condition is not corrected. Changing draw length by altering string length and altering cable extensions are the best ways to make minor adjustments in draw length but are only good for changes less than one inch.

To make **major changes** in draw length you must use a set of wheels of a different size or utilize the multiple draw slots in the eccentric wheel. If your wheels don't have these slots, then you must resort to the more difficult method of changing wheel sizes. Buying new wheels may be an expensive move, but you won't get good results if you are not shooting from the middle of the valley.

The cam wheel system is adjusted using the same methods as for round wheels. The difficult part of the procedure is knowing when you have them adjusted to the middle of the valley.

When you are done adjusting draw length, your wheels should look like those in Figure 64 or Figure 65. If they don't, keep working on them.

Everything that is done to tune the compound bow from this point on is dependent on having the correct draw length. Shooting from the middle of the valley is an absolute must.

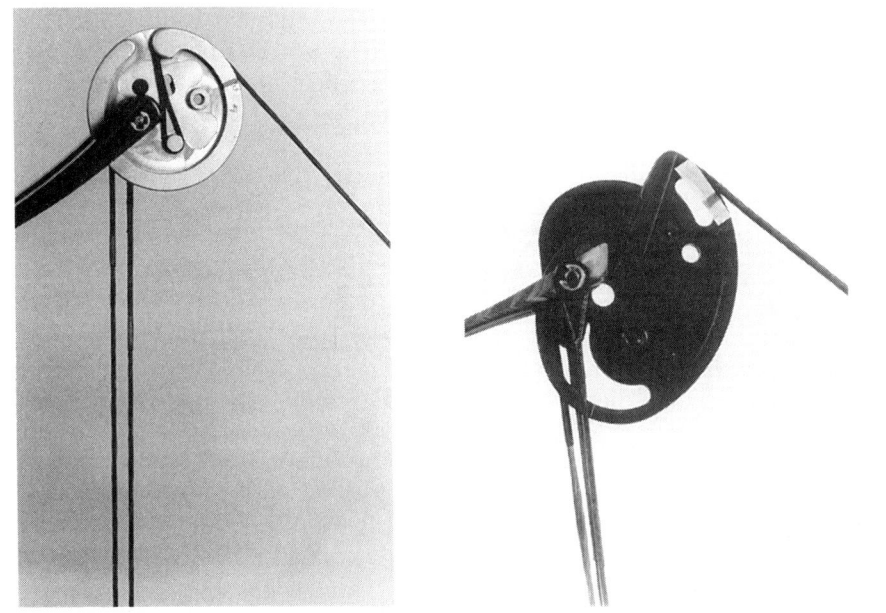

• *Figs. 64 & 65. The middle of the valley is always indicated by the maximum leverage line extending to the point where the cable leaves the wheel.*

Chapter 5
The Power Stroke Of The Compound Bow

A: Comparing Compound And Recurve Bows

The compound bow and the recurve bow have many more similarities than differences, but it is always the differences which stand out in your mind. Both bows have limbs, handles, strings and arrow rests, and they never seem to shoot all of your arrows in the middle of the target. The obvious difference is the use of eccentric wheels on the compound bow. The use of this simple machine on such a simple device as a bow has resulted in nearly a 10 percent increase in speed and, in the hands of the knowledgeable, superior accuracy.

The force-draw curve of the compound has the three main parts of peak, valley and wall. These parts of the curve are produced during the draw cycle of the bow. On the power stroke, after the release of the string, the draw weight of the bow will reverse itself through this force-draw curve. If you are releasing from the middle of the valley, then the weight will smoothly increase out of the valley. As the string moves forward, the draw weight increases until it reaches peak weight. After passing peak, the weight will decrease until the arrow leaves the string.

A comparison of the force-draw curves of compound (Fig. 66) and recurve bows (Fig. 67) reveals the reason for the greater arrow velocities achieved by the compound. Using two bows with the same peak weight, we can first measure the area under each curve to compare their stored energy values. Because the compound reaches peak early in its draw cycle, it stores more energy than the recurve which reaches peak at the end of its draw cycle.

On the release of the recurve bow's string far different conditions occur.

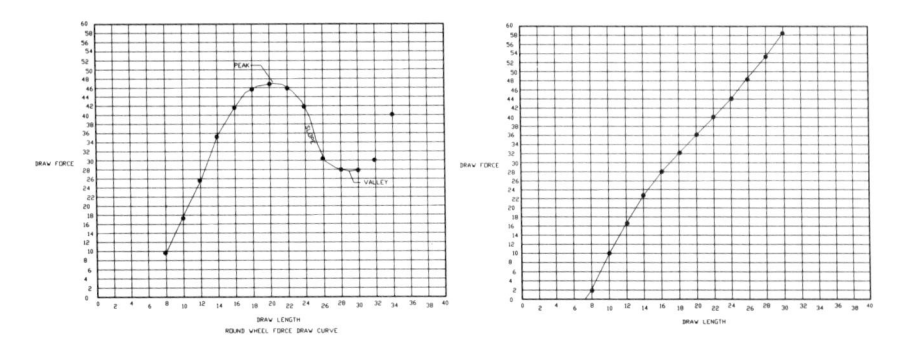

• *Fig. 66, left. The force-draw curve of a compound bow shows the peak weight early in the draw cycle. Fig. 67, right. The recurve force-draw curve shows the peak weight at the end of the draw cycle.*

The recurve string begins at its highest weight and provides a reducing thrust to the arrow. The compound performs in the opposite manner because it begins at a weight that is less than its peak. As the string on the compound moves forward and the weight increases, the arrow is given an increasing thrust. The result is greater velocities being achieved with a compound bow.

B: Why The Cam Bow Should Be Faster

The cam-shaped wheel was designed for the early compounds to provide high levels of stored energy. This is accomplished by making two things happen during the draw cycle. First, the draw weight must increase as quickly as possible and second, the draw weight must stay at peak for as long as possible. The result is a force-draw curve with a near flat spot at peak weight (Fig. 68). More energy is stored under this curve and gives the bow the potential to provide higher speed to the arrow.

Higher speed is not always the only result of the use of cam wheels. Because the draw weight must increase and decrease so quickly, vibrations

• *Fig. 68. The cam wheel generates a curve with a near-flat spot at peak weight.*

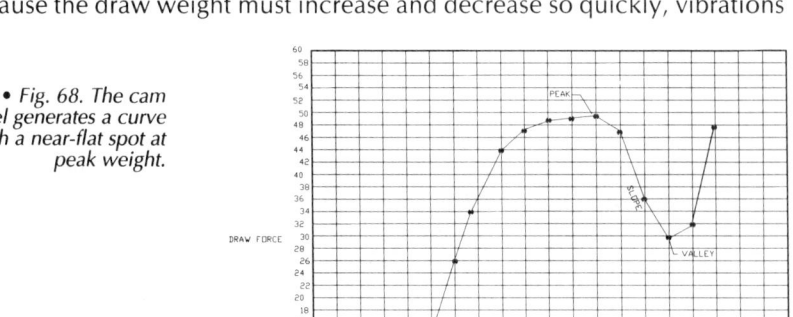

are caused in the cables, limbs and handle riser. These same sharp increases and decreases cause greater vibrations in the arrow which rob it of speed and efficiency. The result may be little extra arrow speed for a lot more work. **Good bow tuning skills are a must if you hope to gain all that you should from the cam bow.**

C: Bow Efficiency

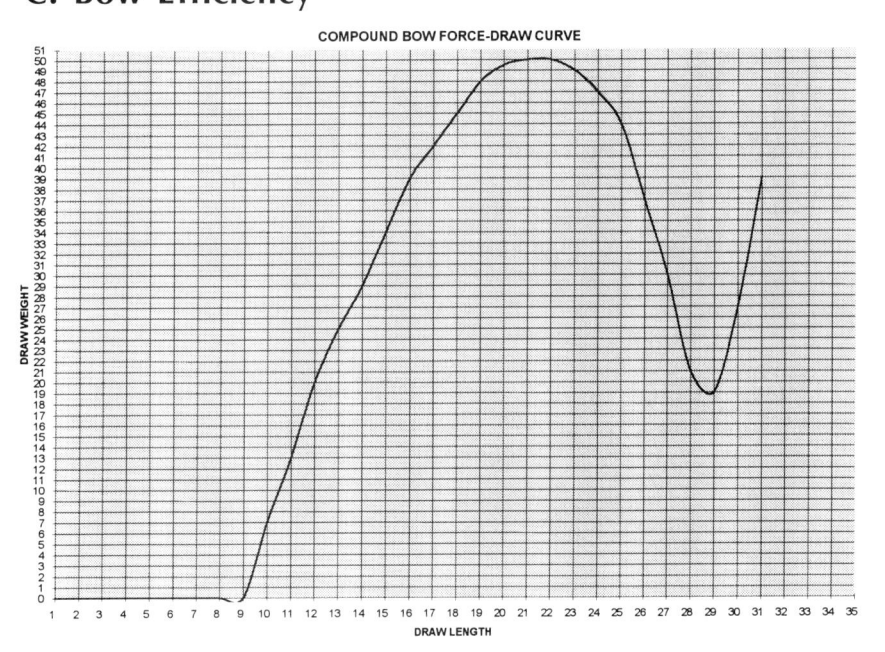

COMPOUND BOW FORCE-DRAW CURVE

DRAW WEIGHT

DRAW LENGTH

• *Fig. 69. The area under the force-draw curve represents stored energy. To calculate the stored energy of the bow, just count the number of small rectangles under the curve, includ-ing – to your best estimate – the relative sizes of each of the partial rectangles below the curve. Each complete rectangle represents one inch-pound of stored energy; divide by 12 to get foot-pounds. Each partial rectangle represents a percentage of one inch-pound of stored energy. Another approximation of stored energy is the sum of the weight measurements from 10 inches draw to 29 inches draw, in this instance; divide by 12 to get foot-pounds.*

"Bow efficiency" is often misunderstood. **Bow or dynamic efficiency is properly defined as the kinetic energy of the arrow divided by the stored energy of the bow, with that efficiency expressed as a percentage.** This efficiency is the measure of how much of the bow's stored energy is transferred to the arrow as the arrow leaves the string.

Recurve and compound bows generally operate in the 60-85 percent level. Many factors influence bow efficiency — design of the bow, weight of the arrow, etc.

The measurement of a bow's efficiency begins with the making of its force-draw curve. Once the curve is made, the area under the curve can be mathematically computed. The area is divided into thin rectangles as in Figure

69. The area of each rectangle is calculated and the sum is taken of all the rectangular areas. In the given example, a bow with a peak weight of 50 pounds, eccentric wheels and a 29-inch draw length will have a stored energy of 57 foot-pounds.

The measurement process is continued by releasing an arrow and recording its velocity. The arrow velocity and arrow weight can then be used in the formula for kinetic energy: **KE = arrow weight in grains x velocity x velocity/450,240.** This gives the kinetic energy in foot-pounds.

In the example at hand, the arrow weight is 500 grains and its initial velocity is 200 feet per second. Applying the formula for kinetic energy, we get 44.42 foot-pounds of energy in the arrow.

The **efficiency** of **this particular bow, shooting this given arrow**, is the result obtained by dividing 44.42 by 57 (KE/stored energy) — in other words, 77.9 percent.

High efficiency does not automatically mean high velocity. To get high velocity you must first store lots of energy. After that has taken place, the bow must transfer most of that energy to the arrow.

D: Bow Performance — The Road To Accuracy

The terms "bow performance" and "bow efficiency" are not the same, although they are related. To me, bow performance is a measure of how often the bow is shooting arrows into the spot of aim. I use a percent value to determine this performance level. If a given bow is hitting the spot of aim nine out of ten times then it earns a ninety percent rating.

Ninety percent in professional archery means you finish out of the money. In bow hunting it means you dig your arrow out of the dirt and try again the next morning.

One hundred percent is where the action is. **The bow must shoot the arrow where it is aimed every time.** If you aim it three inches high it must hit three inches high.

One hundred percent performance is more than difficult to obtain. In fact, I have had only four bows which would get this rating. All of those have been variations on the same two-wheel compound.

Performance depends on the following things:

1) high bow efficiency
2) correct draw length
3) good arrow rest/arrow size combination
4) persistence in the fine tuning process
5) sound design
6) good engineering
7) quality materials

All of these factors must come together in order to achieve perfect performance, and the glue that holds them together is persistence in the fine tuning process. Any one can put the other six items together. Persistence is what gets the bow to that 100% level and 100% performance puts accuracy control in the hands of the shooter.

Chapter 6
The Fine Tuning Process

A: Rechecking The Bow System

Tuning the compound bow to reach maximum reliability begins with the steps outlined in the previous chapters. The finishing touches are contained in this chapter. Fine tuning, as it is called, takes the potential shooting ability of the bow and turns it into real performance. The steps that follow in this chapter make up a method for fine tuning but do not guarantee success. Only persistence and desire to achieve high performance will guarantee success.

Fine tuning begins with a complete check of everything that has been done to the bow thus far. That means you must check the following: 1) top and bottom limb tiller; 2) draw weight; 3) nocking point; 4) center shot; and 5) draw length. With these major adjustments in order it is finally possible to fine tune your bow.

B: Fletch Clearance

The best results in bow tuning are achieved by making the arrow pass by the arrow rest without the feathers or vanes making contact. If the vanes or feathers strike the rest at any time while the arrow is in flight, then the possibility exists that every arrow will fly differently. Obviously, the **first** order of business is to **check for fletch contact with the arrow rest.**

The best way to gain factual data on fletch contact is to spray white powder foot spray on the fletching of the arrow (Fig. 70). Spray the last five or six inches of the fletch end of the arrow with powder and then shoot the arrow into a backstop from close range. If the fletch is making contact with the arrow rest marks will appear on the vanes.

In addition to spraying the arrow you may want to spray the arrow rest and the sight window of the bow (Fig. 71). If the fletching is making contact

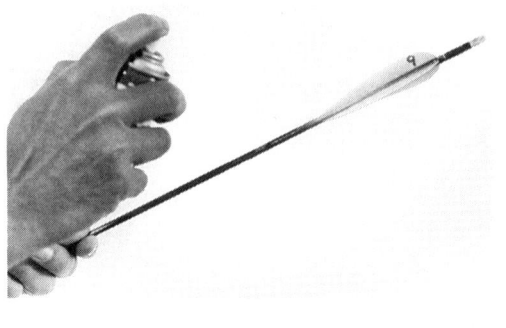

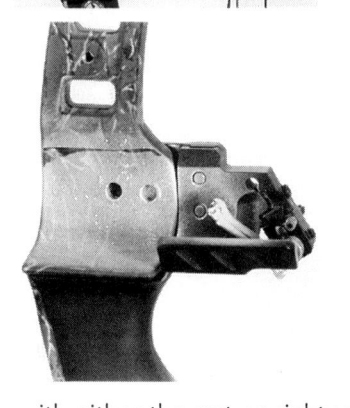

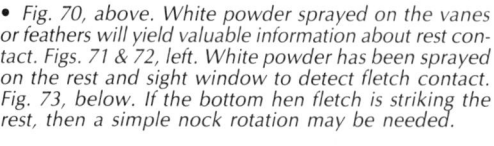

• *Fig. 70, above. White powder sprayed on the vanes or feathers will yield valuable information about rest contact. Figs. 71 & 72, left. White powder has been sprayed on the rest and sight window to detect fletch contact. Fig. 73, below. If the bottom hen fletch is striking the rest, then a simple nock rotation may be needed.*

with either the rest or sight window, some markings should show on the white powder (Fig. 72). In any event, the collection of facts is of primary importance before making adjustments.

Depending on the type and severity of the contact, some changes can eliminate fletch contact with the rest. Severe contact may mean you have to change arrow sizes. Lesser contact can sometimes be eliminated by a simple rotation of the nock on the arrow.

Severe contact of the arrow against the rest means that the arrow is acting too stiff. This may be for several reasons: the arrow may in fact be too stiff, the nock may fit too tight on the bowstring or you may be torquing the string with your fingers while at full draw.

Check the nock fit by holding the bow string horizontal with the arrow hanging downward from the bowstring. Tap the string with your hand. The arrow should fall off the string with a light or medium tap. If it doesn't, try a different size nock.

Work on your finger and wrist position at full draw. If the arrow is still striking the rest, change to a weaker spine arrow shaft.

Light contact between the arrow and the rest can usually be eliminated by placing the nocks on your arrows in a slightly rotated position. Figure 73 shows the bottom hen vane of an arrow which is making contact with a springy rest. In this case, by rotating the nock in the counter-clockwise direction (Fig. 74), the vane can pass farther to the left and miss the end of the rest. The shoot-through rests require that the nock be rotated clockwise (Fig. 75). Don't be afraid to experiment with this technique.

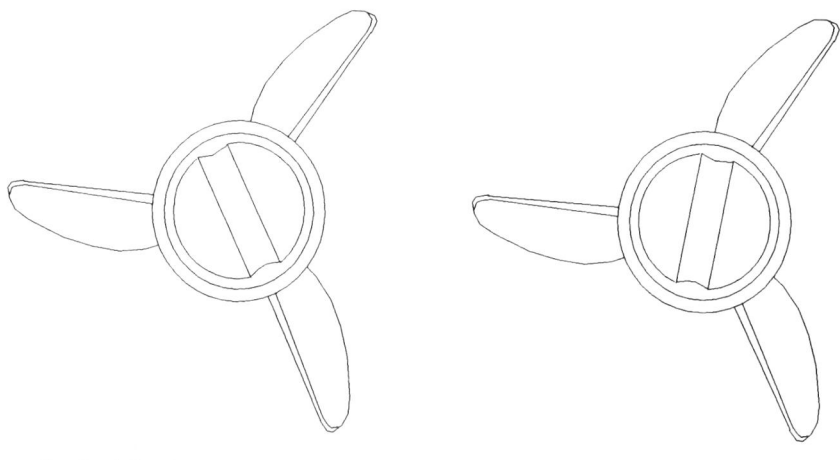

• *Fig. 74, left. This nock is rotated slightly counter-clockwise. Fig. 75, right. This nock is rotated clockwise a few degrees.*

Some contact may never be eliminated. Four-fletched arrows may fall into this category because they have one more feather or vane to pass by the rest. You may have to settle for a small amount of contact between the fletching and the rest, but only if your arrows are grouping well. In this case, feathers will work better than vanes because feathers will give way when making contact with a rest. The final test will be the flight of a broadhead under this condition.

One final suggestion regarding fletch contact with the rest is to check the physical size of your rest. It may be too wide or too thick to allow clear fletch passage (Fig. 76). You may need to bend some parts out of the way or cut some parts to smaller sizes to allow passage of the arrow fletch (Fig. 77).

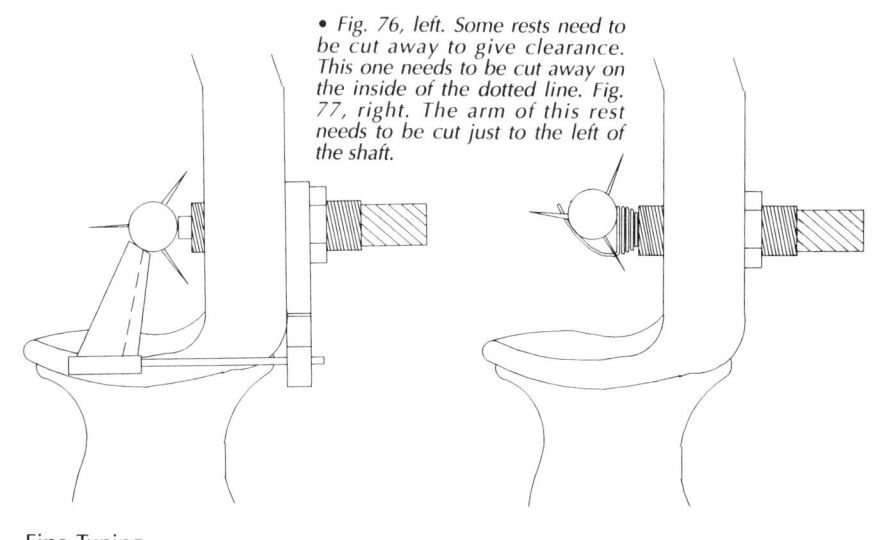

• *Fig. 76, left. Some rests need to be cut away to give clearance. This one needs to be cut away on the inside of the dotted line. Fig. 77, right. The arm of this rest needs to be cut just to the left of the shaft.*

C: Paper Testing

Paper testing is the art of shooting holes in newspaper. I do this with fletched arrows from a distance of three to eight yards. The newspaper is mounted on a picture frame (Fig. 78) and hung one to two yards in front of the target. The purpose is to collect facts about the actual flight of the arrow as it leaves the bow and as it tries to recover from its bending motions caused by the initial thrust of the bow. The tears the arrow makes as it passes through the paper are the record of its flight pattern.

• *Fig. 78. A simple wood frame covered with newspaper will show you how your arrow is leaving the bow.*

As you begin to use this paper test method of tuning it might be good to start close. Shoot from one or two yards in front of the paper. If the results are good, move back two yards and continue testing. When you reach a distance of **about seven or eight yards the arrow is usually showing its worst motion** as it tries to recover from the bending motions created during the power stroke of the bow.

The use of a release aid should give better results than using the traditional finger release. Because the release usually gives a smoother start to the arrow, the holes in the paper are smaller with cleaner vane and feather cuts. **Most finger shooters stay within five yards of the target to avoid seeing rather large holes in the paper.**

1) Nocking point position is the first concern when paper testing. Regardless of shooting style, everyone is looking for the same basic result in the paper.

Right handed shooters should work toward a hole in the paper that is perfect or that shows the **nock slightly high and left** (Fig. 79). A hole that tears slightly nock high is also acceptable. **Left handed shooters** are looking for holes that tear perfectly or slightly **nock high right.** Holes like these indicate that the arrow is rising up and away from the arrow rest. This is a desirable effect because the arrow will not strike the rest on its path by the handle riser. Another advantage of this action is that if the arrow is not riding against the rest then hand movement is not likely to affect the flight of the arrow.

• Fig. 79. From left to right, these holes show a perfect tear, one-fourth inch nock high left, and one-half inch nock high left. Fletches make the long, slender tears; point of entry is at the star-shaped tear. These holes are desirable for right-handed shooters. For left-handed shooters, holes should tear slightly high right.

• Fig. 80, left. Nock end of this arrow is tearing too low and, for a right-handed shooter, too much left. Fig. 81, right. Nock end of this arrow is a little high.

2) Arrows that tear holes with the nock in a downward direction (Fig. 80) are starting with the nock end too low. The remedy is a higher nocking point. If the arrow is tearing a hole with the nock too high in the upward direction (Fig. 81) then the nocking point may be too high. Try moving the nocking point down.

Some shoot-through rests will always give a slight tear upward and usually require a nocking point of 3/16 inches or higher. Reset the nocking point until you get the best results you think are possible, but **be prepared to change it when you begin long distance shooting.** I find that the stiffer the launcher the higher the arrow will tear through the paper. **A rule of thumb is to get a hole that is no more than one-half to three-fourths of an inch nock high.** The final test, as is always the case, will be how well the arrows fly and group at long range.

Arrows that are **weak in spine** for a given draw weight will tear **holes with the nock left** for a **right handed archer** as they pass through the paper (Fig. 82), and a combination of adjustments can help change this condition. (The hole will show **nock right** for a **left handed shooter.** A decrease in draw

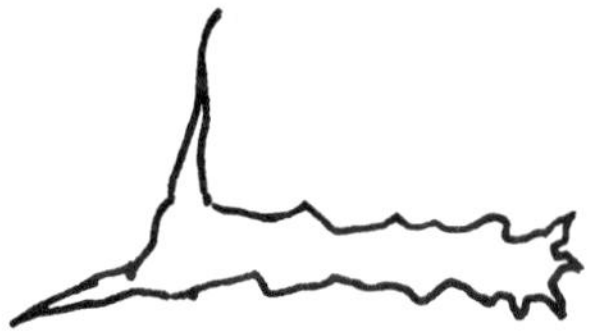

• Fig. 82. For a right handed shooter, a nock left tear indicates a weak acting arrow. Nock tear would be to the right for a left handed shooter.

weight may improve initial flight of the arrow, and an increase in the tension of the cushion plunger may also help. A change in center shot can be made in either direction, but I have experienced little improvement when adjusting center shot on my own bows. The last adjustment to be made is to try several other arrow sizes.

Should your arrows tear **holes to the right** (Fig. 83) as they pass through the paper **(right handed shooter),** then they are **too stiff** in spine and several adjustments are in order. For **left handed shooters,** holes will tear **nock left.**

• Fig. 83. A tear to the right shows an arrow acting stiff for a right handed shooter. For a left handed shooter, the tear would be to the left.

The first change should be to increase the draw weight of the bow. In addition to that, try decreasing the tension of the cushion plunger. By adjusting both weight and plunger tension some improvement can be achieved. You must find a rest which the arrow leaves with less tear to the right or left, depending upon which side you shoot from. Some rests will have that effect. The last resort here is to change to another kind of rest to improve the nock-right or nock-left situation.

A weaker shaft should also show holes that tear less to the right for a right handed shooter and less to the left for a left handed shooter. Changing center shot may also help, so try moving the rest in either direction to obtain better results.

All of these adjustments may or may not improve your arrow flight through the paper. With some experimenting, you should hit upon a combination which gives good results through paper.

From the beginning, you should **be patient and thorough** when paper testing. I do all of my paper testing with fletched arrows that pass by the rest without any fletch contact, and every bow test involves two or three different arrow sizes from several different distances. Without this amount of data you could waste a lot of time shooting from long range to find out what two or three shots through the paper will tell you.

As you will find, the **most difficult situation to eliminate in tuning is that of the stiff arrow.** Without the paper test, many shooters have spent hours tuning and shooting with stiff arrows, getting a good group one end and a bad group the next end. This kind of pattern can cause the shooter too blame himself instead of the equipment mis-match. Inconsistent grouping is the mark of the stiff arrow, but by using the paper test, the right changes can get improved results.

The too-weak arrow usually gives bad arrow flight and bad groups which lead you to some quick changes instead of blaming yourself. Again, the paper test will tell you what the problem is so you can make the right adjustments.

D: Flow Chart For Tuning The Compound Bow

The steps for tuning your bow as set forth in this book are outlined in the following flow chart. Keep this page handy when tuning so you can use this tuning system more effectively.

1) Brand selection
2) Draw length measurement
3) Rest selection and installation
4) Sight selection and installation
5) Tiller setting
6) Draw weight setting
7) Nock point setting

8) Draw length adjustment. If change is made, go to #6.

9) Arrow selection

10) Powder testing. If arrow size is changed, go to #9.
   If rest is changed, go to #7.

11) Paper testing. If arrow size is changed, go to #9.
   If rest is changed, go to #7.
   If nock point is changed, go to #10.
   If center shot is changed, go to #10.

12) Shoot testing, short range. If no groups, go to #7.

13) Shoot testing, long range. If no groups, go to #7.
   If no groups, go to #6.
   If no groups, go to #3.

14) Broadhead testing. If bad flight, go to #10.
   If bad flight, go to #7.
   If bad flight, go to #6.
   If bad flight, go to #3.
   Keep at it until good flight is obtained, then shoot for groups.
   If no groups, go to #7.
   If no groups, go to #6.
   If no groups, go to #3.
   Persistence pays off eventually!!!!!

Chapter 7
Test Shooting — The Final Step
A: Target Point And Field Point Testing

Shoot testing is the final step in fine tuning your compound bow. The results that are obtained here will determine whether or not you need to go back to a previous step and readjust several things. The groups you shoot are always the last word in bow hunting.

The shooting process **begins at short range** — 15 or 20 yards. At close range you can adjust your sight pins, adjust your peep sight and test the feel of the draw length. This distance gives you a chance to become familiar with a new bow or readjust to an old bow you have changed. If your arrows are not grouping here at 20 yards then it is necessary to make changes in nocking point location, type of arrow rest, arrow size and maybe even draw length. In other words, you will have to backtrack several steps in the tuning process and rebuild your bow.

It is important to point out at this time that **tuning requires patience and repetition** of the steps outlined so far in this book. Without that patience and persistence you may not get your bow tuned. Don't expect results overnight.

Many shooters like to try shooting bare shafts at close range. Finger shooters stay at about five yards while release shooters go as far back as 20 yards. The result should be the same as the paper test. If your arrow is tearing a hole slightly nock high left (right handed shooter) through the paper (Fig. 84), then the bare shaft should shoot to low and right, which indicates that the nock end is still high left. Left handed shooter will have nocks high right. **The paper test tells you what the back of the arrow is doing while the bare shaft tells what the front of the arrow is doing, so the two tests show opposite results.** If they don't, then recheck for fletch contact with the arrow rest. The desirable bare shaft test for right handed shooters will result in the

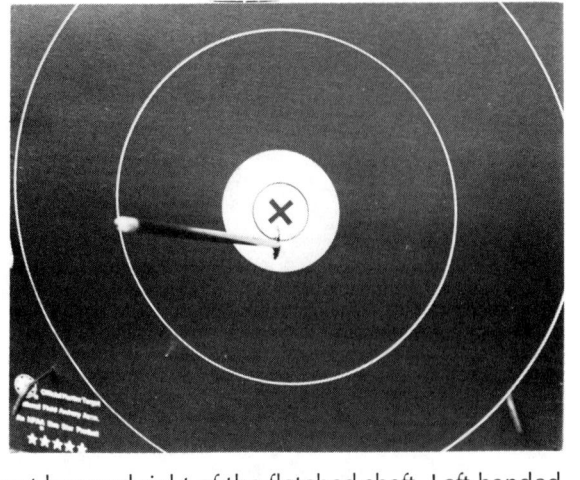

• *Fig. 84. If the nock end of the arrow is tearing high through paper, then the bare shaft will shoot low.*

shaft point hitting the target low and right of the fletched shaft. Left handed shooters will have the shaft point hitting low and left of the fletched shaft.

Once you meet with some success at close range with fletched arrows, move to 40 or 50 yards. The distance you choose should reflect your skill level; don't overdo it and frustrate yourself. Long range shooting should give you a clear look at arrow flight and a better picture of arrow groups. If arrow flight is not good, alter arrow rest and shaft until better results are obtained.

At longer distances, the final adjustments to nocking point and rest tensions are made. Moving the nocking point one-sixteenth of an inch can make a big difference in some bows, so do a lot of shooting with the nocking point in different locations until you get the best groups. The same is true of plunger tension and launcher tension.

My experience has shown that if I am getting groups which seem to be across the target face, then I should move the nocking point up the string and/or decrease the plunger tension. If the groups you are getting are up and down (Fig. 85) on the target face, then move the nocking point down the string and/or increase the plunger tension (Fig. 86). These rules are by no means guaranteed to work all of the time, but they do give you a systematic approach to follow. **Don't be afraid to try adjusting in the opposite direction of what is ''supposed'' to work.**

Whenever you are not getting the results you would like, back up in the tuning process and try another rest, recheck your draw length and try another size arrow shaft. You may pull out some of your hair after awhile, but if you stick at it long enough, the results will start to show. I have on occasion spent from daylight until dark tuning a single bow and still couldn't hit the spot with it. On the next day, you may try that one idea that eluded you previously and finally get the results you wanted. Tuning is not easy if your expectations are high.

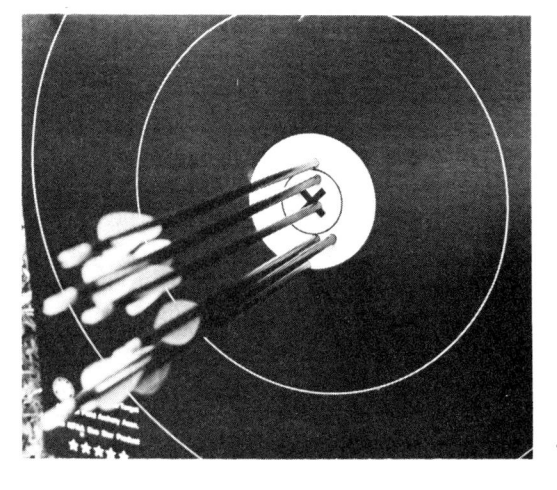

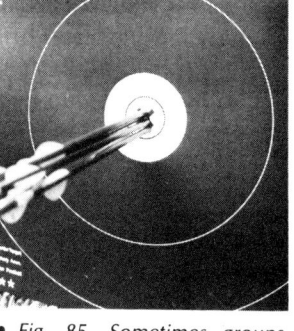

• *Fig. 85. Sometimes groups which are vertical can be corrected by a nocking point change. Fig. 86, above. This is the kind of group possible when all is working well.*

B: Setting Your Own Accuracy Goals

Shooting at the professional level requires consistent accuracy on a four-inch dot at 50 yards, but most readers of this book will have a different long range shooting goal. **The goal that you set for yourself depends on your purpose.** If hunting is your only activity, perhaps you want to put every arrow in a paper plate at 35 yards. If you are just starting archery, move the paper plate to 20 yards. The experienced shooter may want to hit the paper plate every time at 50 yards. **Be realistic** in your shooting goals so you don't frustrate yourself.

C: Broadhead Tuning

About two weeks before season opens each year, we all have the same objective — shooting broadheads accurately. This age-old ritual is what binds the many facets of archery together, and yet it also drives us crazy. For weeks and maybe months we have been tuning and shooting and meeting with some success. But now, we can't hit anything just because we put a couple of little wings on the front end of our arrows.

Tuning the broadhead involves an added dimension. This dimension is the set of wings on the lead end of the arrow. Wings on the front end make a somewhat unstable projectile unless bigger wings are placed on the back end of the arrow shaft.

Clearly, broadhead accuracy depends on which end is controlling the flight of the arrow. If the front end of the arrow is steering, the arrow could end up anywhere. If the back end of the arrow has sufficient wing surface and

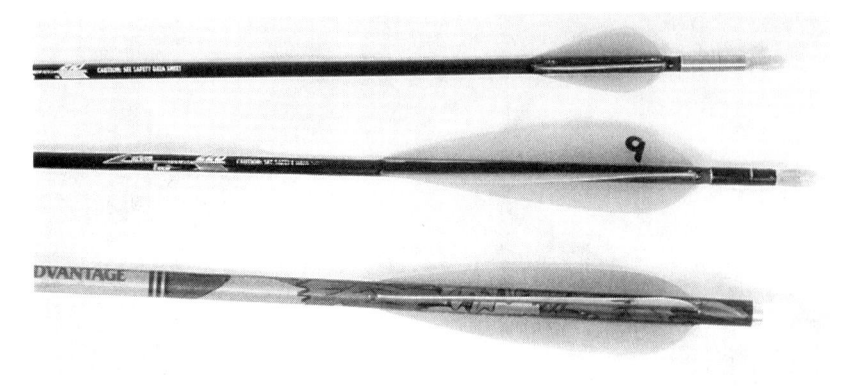

• *Fig. 87. Long fletching with a helical curve, center arrow, will stabilize broadheads.*

if that surface is installed with a helical clamp to give more air resistance (Fig. 87), the back of the arrow will have a better chance to steer the shaft.

The best accuracy would be achieved by putting two blades with small surface area on the front of an arrow and six or eight large fletches on the back of the shaft. Small blade area on the broadhead would mean less steering capability on the front of the shaft, while many fletches on the back would give the best steering possible to the rear of the shaft. This extreme example would be extremely slow in flight, so most of us use some less radical combination of fletch and blade area.

The steering ability of vanes is less than that of feathers of equal size. The ribbed side of the feather creates more drag than the smooth side of an equal-sized vane and stabilizes an arrow quicker. Feathers also are more forgiving of errors you may make in release. For these reasons, many bowhunters prefer the feathered arrow. Vanes, on the other hand, don't absorb water in the rain, are quieter in the quiver and are more durable. These features make the vane popular.

Regardless of the type of fletch you use, **it is important to have enough and the right size vanes or feathers on the arrow shaft to control a broadhead.** I prefer three vanes, four to five inches long, placed on the shaft with either a right helical or left helical curve. Five-inch fletches are the safest. The direction of the curve is not important; just make sure that all the fletches have the same curve. Four fletches will stabilize the arrow quicker than three, but I like to be sure that all fletches are clearing the rest without making contact. If four fletches are working well for you then don't change. The more fletching surface area you put on your arrows, the quicker the arrow will stabilize.

The **size of blades** on the broadhead has a **direct effect on the flight of the arrow.** More blade area makes the arrow harder to guide and requires more fletching on the back of the arrow shaft. Smaller blade area is not as hard to control.

Broadhead weight also has an effect on arrow performance. By placing more weight on the point end, you are causing the arrow to act weaker in spine. This weaker spine shows up as more bending motion in the arrow and may cause the arrow to be harder to stabilize. Be reasonable . . . put lighter broadheads on light arrows and heavier broadheads on heavy arrows.

The **most difficult situation** to control is the **broadhead** that is **not mounted straight on the shaft.** This is common among broadheads and great care must be taken to install each point so it is straight. A good method for doing this is to roll your arrow in an arrow straightener (Fig. 88) and visually

• *Fig. 88. Check for broadhead alignment straightness by rotating your arrow in a straightener to check for point wobble.*

check to see if the point spins without a wobble. If it wobbles, try heating the shaft enough to loosen the glue, and then reset the point in the end of the shaft. This often will get the point straight. Sometimes you might have to try another lock ring on the point or a different broadhead. If broadheads are not all straight, then it makes no sense tuning the bow because they will all shoot differently.

From this point on, the tuning process is the same as it was with target points. **The broadhead will uncover some problems that were not showing up before, because the broadhead will cause the arrow to perform differently.** Don't hesitate to change the nocking point, draw weight, rest tensions or arrow sizes. Only the very lucky don't have to tune their broadheads differently from their field points.

Be sure to sight in your bow with quiver and arrows attached to the bow (Fig. 89) if you hunt with a bow quiver. Usually, the arrows will strike at a slightly different point when the quiver and arrows are installed. Also make sure you **have all of your silencing devices installed.** Keep checking your sights by shooting at least one arrow before each hunt.

I complete the tuning of my hunting bow with the same test I give my best tournament bows. I shoot my broadheads at a four-inch dot from 50 yards. Your goal may be different, but you expect to see the same good flight that I do. Testing three or four arrows with broadheads should still show good groups (Fig. 90) but the final test is bagging that eight-point buck.

• *Fig. 90. Broadheads may group in a different spot than field points. You won't know until you practice with them. You don't want to miss a trophy, or any target, because you failed to set up and check your equipment.*

• *Fig. 89. Make sure you install quiver, arrows and silencing equipment before sighting and tuning broadheads.*

Shoot Testing

Chapter 8

Tuning The Fast Flight Cable System

A) Introduction

The Fast Flight bow string has been on the market for several years and has made a significant contribution to archery. Its properties of light weight and high damping capabilities have increased arrow velocities and bow consistency. The high strength of this new string material allows it to be used on cam bows as well as on round wheel bows. It can be used as a bowstring and as a replacement for wire cables. Because Fast Flight helps to dampen the vibrations within the compound system, the noise levels of wheel bows and cam bows is reduced. It also resists cutting and fraying, which means it will take plenty of abuse on a hunting bow.

The material itself is high performance polyethylene. The developer, DSM of the Netherlands, engineered a process which arranges the polyethylene molecules so they are parallel. This feature of Dyneema SK60, the development name, gives it properties that can't be attained by any other method.

Dyneema SK60 has the greatest specific strength of any man-made fiber and is the only man-made fiber with low enough density to float on water. It is highly resistant to chemicals such as hydrochloric acid, gasoline and kerosene, as well as salt water and plain water. Dyneema SK60 combines the properties of high strength, low elongation, low weight and high durability. It has excellent resistance to light, resistance to abrasion, good flex life and great damping ability.

Jim Pickering, who has tested and developed Fast Flight systems for Hoyt, supplied me with technical information on Dyneema SK60. In tests he conducted, the cables and string withstood 1,500 dry firings on a 70-pound bow with no failure. After 300,000 cycles of a Fast Flight system, the only sign of wear was at the point where the two cables rubbed against each other, and this was minimal. At one hundred shots a day, this system would last for well over eight years with little or no wear.

One fault of Fast Flight is the slippery surface of the strands. This condition can allow the center serving to slide up the bowstring after some use. This, however, can be overcome by increasing the length of center serving above your nocking point to about three inches. The added length of serving will prevent the nocking point from moving.

When Fast Flight is used for the power cables on a compound bow, some changes occur:
  • The high damping capability of this material will reduce the noise level of your bow.
  • The omission of the tear-drop string anchor from the cable system is another change. Replacing cables is extremely easy since the Fast Flight system hooks onto an anchor pin on the wheel. Its most important effect is the consistency it gives to the compound system.

As you continue to use this new style cable system, you realize that when twisting the cables to change their length you also control eccentric timing and draw length. One twist on one cable will have a small but noticeable effect on the eccentric timing and draw length. This change may be enough to improve your aiming of the bow and grouping of arrows shot from your bow.

Not all eccentric wheels are designed to receive a Fast Flight cable system. To use a cable made from Fast Flight, an anchor pin must be provided on the wheel (Fig. 91). The served loop on the end of the string cable is then hooked over the anchor provision. The string cable is then wrapped around the wheel, and its other end is attached to the axle of the other wheel. In some cases, the other end is attached to the yoke harness which is hooked to the axle. In either case, an anchor provision on the wheel is required.

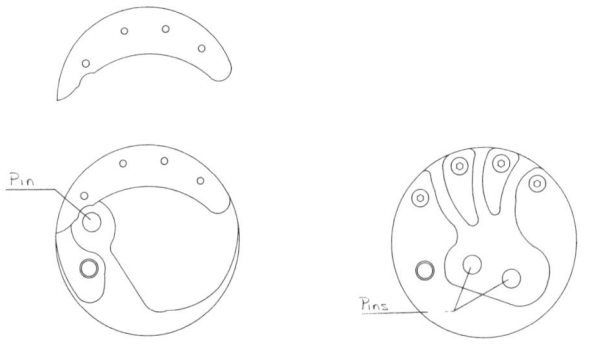

  • Fig. 91. This eccentric has two loop anchor pins on the bow string side of the wheel and one pin on the cable side. Changing either string or cable requires the use of some kind of bow press and can be done in three or four minutes.

Tuning The Fast Flight Cable System

B) Installation

The installation of a Fast Flight cable system involves two simple steps. First, the string cables must be the proper length and the needed servings must be in place. Next, the strings should be twisted to obtain the draw length you need and to set eccentric synchronization.

The length of the string cables should be about one-fourth inch shorter than the desired finished length. This will allow the tension of the limbs to bring the string to its shooting length. Remember, a Fast Flight string will only increase in length about 1/4 inch after installation. This is due to some stretching and slipping that takes place.

Care must be taken when building the Fast Flight cable system. I recommend using 18 or 20 strands in the cables. The end servings should be of braided Fast Flight serving thread, and should be long enough to extend around the wheel plus about two inches. The serving will help retard wear as the cable wraps and unwraps around the wheel with each shot.

After one end of the cable has been attached to the wheel, put 20 to 30 twists in the cable. This procedure will prevent minor frays on individual strands and increase the strength of the material. In fact, strength increases until the number of twists exceeds 100 per meter.

Before the cables are placed on the wheels, be sure to remove any burrs or sharp edges from the wheel. A small rat-tail file can be used for this purpose. This sequence of steps should be done while the bow is in a bow press and the wheels removed. Once all edges are smoothed, install the string cables on the wheels.

To prevent wear on the cables, it may be a good idea to use a plastic cable slide device on your cable guard. Most bows come equipped with this little item. The slide has two grooves which receive the cables and keep them from rubbing against the metal cable guard. I have used one on my own Fast Flight system for thousands of shots and have had only positive results.

Like the cables, the Fast Flight bow string must be made with care. A Number 18 center serving on 18 strands will make 1/4 or 9/32 inch nocks fit correctly. More strands or heavier serving will require the use of bigger nocks. The end servings of braided Fast Flight should be long enough to wrap completely around the wheel, while the center serving should extend about three inches above the nocking point.

When all cables and the bow string are in place, release the bow press slowly. Make sure that all strings are seating in the wheel groves as the limbs increase the tension of them.

At this point you are ready to begin tuning the eccentric wheel system.

C) Eccentric Wheel Synchronization

If the two Fast Flight cables are not the same length, twists must be added to or subtracted from one of the cables to balance the eccentric roll-over. One way of determining if the wheels are synchronized is to look at the position of each wheel relative to the limb. The limbs should cover the same part on both wheels. If not, an adjustment is necessary.

The best test for eccentric synchronization is to examine the wheels at full draw as shown in Figure 92. For this test, the bow string should be drawn in the center and not at the nocking point. In all probability your wheels will look like Fig. 93 or Fig. 94.

Figure 93 shows the top wheel rolling more than the bottom wheel, while

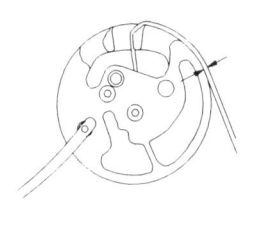 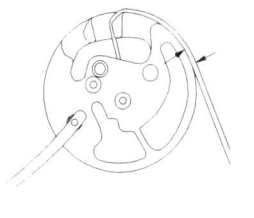 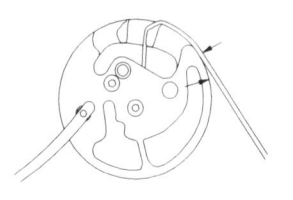

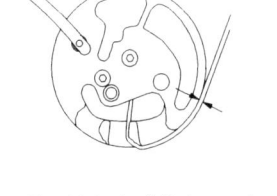 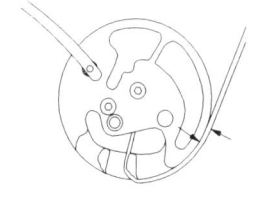 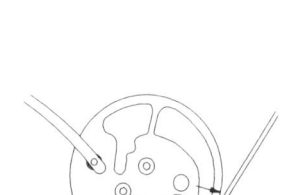

• *Fig. 92A. At full draw, the bow string should be leaving both wheels at the same place in order to have synchroniz-ed roll-over and a smooth shooting bow. The timing marks (indicated by arrows on the wheels) indicate when, as in this drawing, the middle of the valley has been reached.*

• *Fig. 92B. When the bow is underdrawn, the eccen-tric wheels look like this drawing. The timing marks on the wheels have not rolled far enough to reach the middle of the valley.*

• *Fig. 92C. In this drawing, the timing marks have been drawn too far and have pass-ed the middle of the valley.*

Fig. 94 shows the bottom wheel rolling more than the top wheel. These con-ditions are easily corrected by twisting or untwisting the cables.

To adjust the eccentric positions in Fig. 93 you need only to add one or two twists to the cable attached to the anchor pin on the top wheel, or remove one or two twists on the cable attached to the bottom wheel. Add-ing twists to a cable will make it shorter which, in turn, increases draw length. Removing twists will, of course, make the cable longer and draw length shorter.

The wheels in Fig. 94 require the opposite adjustments. Add twists to the cable attached to the bottom wheel or untwist the top wheel cable. If the

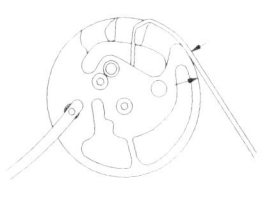

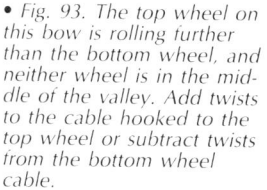

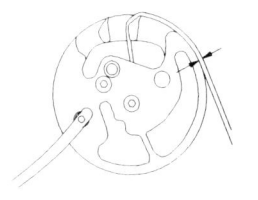

• Fig. 93. The top wheel on this bow is rolling further than the bottom wheel, and neither wheel is in the middle of the valley. Add twists to the cable hooked to the top wheel or subtract twists from the bottom wheel cable.

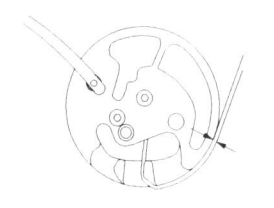

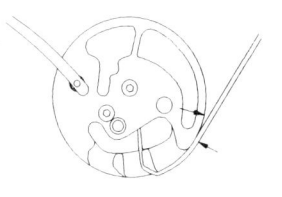

• Fig. 94. In this illustration, the bottom wheel is rolling further than the top wheel. Subtract twists from the cable hooked to the top wheel or add twists to the cable hooked to the bottom wheel.

wheel balance is really bad, do a combination of both adjustments. Remember, the wheels will tell you when you are making the right adjustments and when you are not. Just check Fig. 92 to determine if your wheels are synchronized.

D) Adjusting Draw Length

After the wheels have been synchronized, adjust the draw length of the bow to match your draw length. There are four ways to do this:
1) twisting the bow string,
2) twisting both cables equally,
3) using different string anchor pins and string slots on the wheel and,
4) using a different size wheel.

Major adjustments to draw length are made by placing the bow string in different slots and hooking it to different pins. The rule to remember here: The more string between the two wheels, the more draw length you will have. The two drawings here show a wheel adjusted to the shortest position and to the longest position. The longest position lets as much string as possible out of the wheel so the length of string between the wheels is maximized. The shortest position pulls as much string into the wheel as possible and minimizes the length of string between the wheels.

It is important to note here that the string does not have to be positioned the same in both wheels. You may adjust one end of the string only. This adjustment changes the amount of string between the two wheels but does not change the eccentric synchronization. After each adjustment, check and reset the nocking point to its original setting because it will move up or down depending upon which end of the string is adjusted.

Changing the length of your bow string can also change the draw length. A longer bow string will increase draw length, while a shorter string will decrease draw length. A change of one-half inch in string length will yield about a 3/4 inch change in draw length. If such a change is not enough to match your draw length, and you have exhausted all the adjustments on the wheel, you should consider using a wheel of a different size.

Altering the length of both cables also will adjust draw length. Adding the same number of twists to each cable will shorten the cable but increase the draw length. Removing twists will shorten the draw length. Once the eccentrics are synchronized, the cables must always be twisted equally so synchronization is maintained.

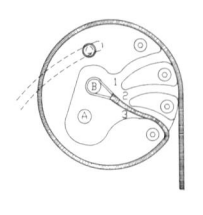

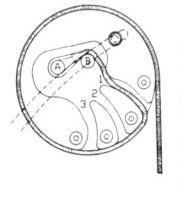

• *Shortest Draw. The slots nearer to the limb tip will give the least amount of draw length. The pin that pulls more string into the interior of the wheel will give less draw length also. This illustration shows the shortest possible draw length available on this wheel.*

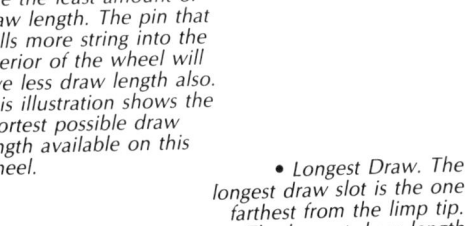

• *Longest Draw. The longest draw slot is the one farthest from the limp tip. The longest draw length available on this wheel is shown in this illustration.*

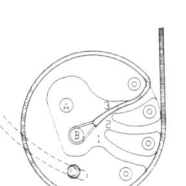

E) Tuning Procedure

After the Fast Flight cables have been adjusted and the string placed in the correct position for your draw length, your bow can be tuned the same as any other compound bow. Begin this by setting your nocking point on the string and powder testing the arrow for total fletch clearance.

During the test shooting phase of tuning, try different adjustments to your Fast Flight cables to improve the groups you are getting. One of the adjustments should be to add one or two twists to one of the power cables. By retesting for groups at 50 yards, you should see a difference. If groups and aiming are worse, try removing one or two twists. Try doing the same to the opposite cable. Collecting this kind of information will enable you to find the wheel balance which produces best arrow grouping for you and your bow.

Try adjustments to the draw length of the bow. This can be done in small increments by adding or subtracting an equal number of twists to each cable. Doing this systematically will help you find the draw length setting which allows you to shoot your best.

Chapter 9
Building And Tuning Arrows

A) Introduction

Once the bow is tuned, the next logical task in equipment preparation is arrow selection. Your choice of arrow involves the traditional aluminum tubular shaft versus the newer carbon tubular shaft. Both make excellent choices for hunting or target shooting if you follow the simple guidelines in this chapter.

If you intend to build your own arrows, use the procedure given later in this chapter. Read the procedure several times. Keep it handy when you begin building arrows. Skipping steps or rushing through any part of the procedure will give you less than the best results, so be thorough.

B) Size Selection

There is one very simple rule to follow when selecting the size of arrow you should shoot: **the size which flies and groups the best out of your bow while you are shooting it is the right size.**

This rule works all the time. Any other rule or chart or crystal ball will not give you the best all the time. Arrow size charts are certainly a source of good information, but don't think that they will give you the one, exact size for you and your bow. Charts are intended to give you a small group of sizes that should work well. Test shooting will be the final criterion for determining which size works best.

Printed in the next few pages are several manufacturers' size selection and comparison charts. When looking at them, you must select two, three or four sizes that are spined and weighted for your draw weight and let off. Borrow arrows of the apparent best sizes for you from members of your club or from a pro shop — if they will let you — and test them at both short and long ranges to determine which groups the best.

I know that not everyone is near a club or a pro shop. That makes it difficult to test several sizes before you buy. In such cases, select a size which favors the heavier weight and spine, whether it be carbon or aluminum. The heavier shaft is usually more stable, quieter and less prone to erratic flight. Speed is important, but remember that **a fast miss is still a miss and a noisy bow brings home no meat.**

CARBON TECH SPINE AND GRAIN WEIGHT CHART		
Shaft Size	Spine Deflection	Grains per Inch
180	1070	5.87
188	900	6.63
196	800	7.30
210	600	8.06
220	500	8.90
230	410	9.75
240	340	10.65

* In the Carbon Tech Size – Spine - Grain Weight chart, the arrow size and spine values are recorded in thousandths of an inch, i.e., the 210 shaft has an outside diameter of .210 inches and its spine deflection or bending amount when weighted in the middle is .600 inches. To calculate arrow weight, multiply arrow length by the number of grains per inch and add the weight of any nock, point and fletch accessories.

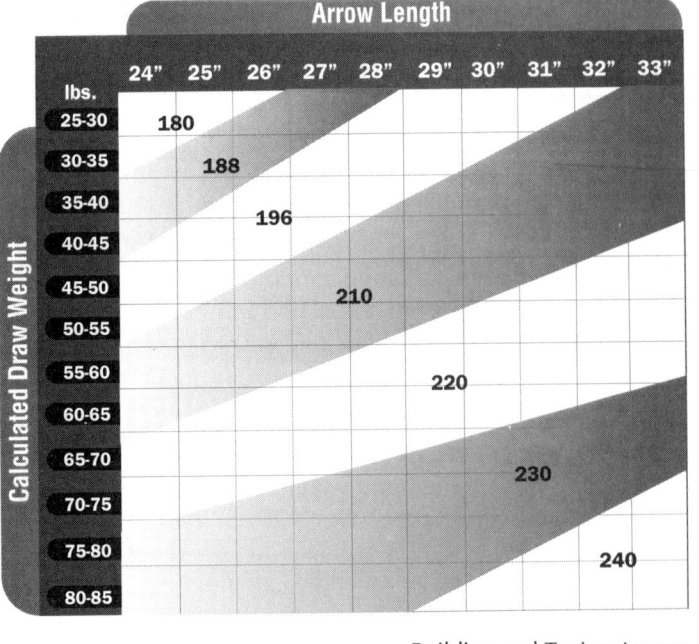

Building and Tuning Arrows

* To select your appropriate arrow size for all-carbon shafts find your calculated bow weight by the computational method in the chart. Use that bow weight and your arrow length to cross-reference the arrow size you need in the Size Selection Chart. If you are borderline between two shaft sizes, choose the heavier size for best results. For example, the proper shaft size for a calculated bow weight of 55-60 pounds and 30 inches in length (from bottom of nock groove to end of shaft) is the 220 shaft. The shaft alone will have a spine value of 500, or .5 inches, and weigh 30 x 8.90 = 267 grains. When tuning your carbon shafts, remember to start with the full-length weight pin and work down from there. Retest after breaking one weight segment from the pin until you find the weight that works best for your setup.

CARBON TECH ARROW SELECTION CHART

Peak Draw Weight	=	
Arrow Length 26.0" or more	+4	
Arrow Length 25.9" or less	-4 =	
Recurve Bow	+6	
Round Wheel	0	
Mild Cam	+6	
Hard Cam	+10 =	
65-80% Let-off	-5	
50% Let-off	0	
35% Let-off	+5 =	
Fast Flight	+5	
Dacron	0 =	
Release Aid	0	
Finger Release	+4 =	
Glue in point below 70 grains	-9	
Glue in point between 70 and 80 grains	-8	
Glue in point between 80 and 90 grains	-7	
Glue in point 100 grains	-6	
Glue in point 125 grains	-4	
Adapter + 100 grain point	-3	
Adapter + 125 grain point	0	
Adapter + 145 grain point	+4 =	
Add/Subtract to determine your calculated bow weight =		

Determining **Correct Arrow Length**
Arrow length is measured from the bottom of the nock groove to the end of the shaft

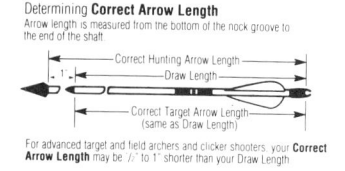

For advanced target and field archers and clicker shooters, your **Correct Arrow Length** may be 1/2" to 1" shorter than your Draw Length

Determining Draw Length
Length from bottom of the nock groove to the front side of the bow while at comfortable full draw.

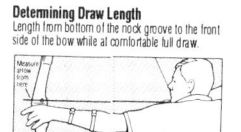

Building and Tuning Arrows

EASTON HUNTING

Bow Weight Selection

RECURVE BOW — Actual or Calculated Bow Weight (Pounds)					COMPOUND BOW — Actual or Calculated Peak Bow Weight (Pounds)				
Broadhead or Field Point Weight Only					Broadhead or Field Point Weight Only				
75 (GRAINS)	100 (GRAINS)	125 (GRAINS)	150 (GRAINS)	175 (GRAINS)	75 (GRAINS)	100 (GRAINS)	125 (GRAINS)	150 (GRAINS)	175 (GRAINS)
65-85	90-110	115-135	140-160	165-185	65-85	90-110	115-135	140-160	165-185
30-34	27-31	24-28	21-25	18-22	35-40	32-37	29-34	26-31	23-28
35-39	32-36	29-33	26-30	23-27	41-46	38-43	35-40	32-37	29-34
40-44	37-41	34-38	31-35	28-32	47-52	44-49	41-46	38-43	35-40
45-49	42-46	39-43	36-40	33-37	53-58	50-55	47-52	44-49	41-46
50-54	47-51	44-48	41-45	38-42	59-64	56-61	53-58	50-55	47-52
55-59	52-56	49-53	46-50	43-47	65-70	62-67	59-64	56-61	53-58
60-64	57-61	54-58	51-55	48-52	71-76	68-73	65-70	62-67	59-64
65-69	62-66	59-63	56-60	53-57	77-82	74-79	71-76	68-73	65-70
70-74	67-71	64-68	61-65	58-62	83-88	80-85	77-82	74-79	71-76
75-79	72-76	69-73	66-70	63-67	89-94	86-91	83-88	80-85	77-82
80-84	77-81	74-78	71-75	68-72	95-100	92-97	89-94	86-91	83-88

> This shaft selection chart was set up using Fast Flite® String, finger release and modern, efficient recurve and compound bows. The shaft size recommendations for compound bows were determined using 40-65% let-off and round wheels. If your equipment varies from the above, see the EASTON BOWHUNTING brochure to determine your Calculated Bow Weight or Calculated Peak Bow Weight before using this chart.

Shaft Selection by Arrow Length (Shaft Size / Model / Weight)

Column headers: 21½"–22" (-22½"), 22½"–23" (-23½"), 23½"–24" (-24½"), 24½"–25" (-25½"). Shaft sizes in **bold** are the most widely used.

Recurve wt.	22" (Size / Model / Wt)	23" (Size / Model / Wt)	24" (Size / Model / Wt)	25" (Size / Model / Wt)
(lightest)				1813 / XX75 / 197 A
30-34			1813 / XX75 / 189 A	1913 / XX75 / 209 A
35-39			1816 / XX75,E / 232 A	1816 / XX75,E / 232 A; 3L-04 / A/C/C / 173
40-44		1813 / XX75 / 181 A; 1816 / XX75,E / 223 A; 3L-04 / A/C/C / 167	1913 / XX75 / 200 A; 1816 / XX75,E / 223 A; 1818 / XX75 / 268 A; 3L-04 / A/C/C / 180	1913 / XX75 / 209 B; 2013 / XX75 / 225 A; 3-04 / A/C/C / 180
45-49	1813 / XX75 / 173 A; 1816 / XX75,E / 213 A; 3L-04 / A/C/C / 160	1913 / XX75 / 192 A; 1816 / XX75,E / 213 A; 3-04 / A/C/C / 173	1913 / XX75 / 200 B; 1916 / XX75,E / 223 A; 1818 / XX75 / 257 A; 3L-18 / A/C/C / 186	2013 / XX75 / 225 A; 1916 / XX75,E / 251 A; 1818 / XX75 / 268 B; 3L-18 / A/C/C / 186
50-54	1913 / XX75 / 184 A; 1816 / XX75,E / 204 A; 3L-04 / A/C/C / 153	1913 / XX75 / 192 B; 1916 / XX75,E / 213 B; 1818 / XX75 / 246 A; 3-04 / A/C/C / 166	2013 / XX75 / 216 A; 1916 / XX75,E / 241 A; 1918 / XX75 / 257 B; 3L-18 / A/C/C / 179	2013 / XX75 / 225 B; 1916 / XX75,E / 251 B; 1918 / XX75 / 290 A; 3L-18 / A/C/C / 186; 3-18 / A/C/C / 195
55-59	1913 / XX75 / 184 B; 1816 / XX75,E / 235 A; 1818 / XX75 / 235 A; 3-04 / A/C/C / 158	2013 / XX75 / 207 A; 1916 / XX75,E / 231 A; 1918 / XX75 / 246 B; 3L-18 / A/C/C / 172; 3-18 / A/C/C / 187	2013 / XX75 / 216 B; 1916 / XX75,E / 241 B; 1918 / XX75 / 278 A; 3L-18 / A/C/C / 179	2113 / XX75 / 233 A; 2016 / XX75 / 264 A; 1918 / XX75 / 290 B; 3-18 / A/C/C / 195
60-64	2013 / XX75 / 198 A; 1916 / XX75,E / 221 A; 1818 / XX75 / 235 B; 3L-18 / A/C/C / 164	2013 / XX75 / 207 B; 1916 / XX75,E / 231 B; 1918 / XX75 / 266 A; 3L-18 / A/C/C / 180; 3-18 / A/C/C / 180	2113 / XX75 / 223 A; 2016 / XX75 / 253 A; 2018 / XX75 / 278 B; 3-18 / A/C/C / 187	2113 / XX75 / 233 C; 2114 / XX75 / 247 C; 2115 / XX75 / 269 A; 2018 / XX75,E / 307 A; 3-30 / A/C/C / 202
65-69	2013 / XX75 / 198 B; 1916 / XX75,E / 221 B; 1918 / XX75 / 255 A; 3L-18 / A/C/C / 164; 3-18 / A/C/C / 172	2113 / XX75 / 214 A; 2016 / XX75 / 253 B; 1918 / XX75 / 266 B; 3-18 / A/C/C / 180	2113 / XX75 / 223 C; 2114 / XX75 / 237 B; 2115 / XX75 / 259 A; 2018 / XX75,E / 282 B; 3-30 / A/C/C / 194	2213 / XX75 / 246 A; 2114 / XX75 / 247 C; 2115 / XX75 / 269 B; 2020 / XX75 / 337 A; 3-30 / A/C/H / 202
70-74	2016 / XX75 / 226 A; 1918 / XX75 / 255 B; 2018 / XX75,E / 282 A; 3-18 / A/C/C / 172	2113 / XX75 / 221 B; 2016 / XX75 / 232 B; 2115 / XX75 / 248 B; 2018 / XX75,E / 282 B; 3-30 / A/C/C / 186	2114 / XX75 / 237 C; 2115 / XX75 / 259 B; 2018 / XX75 / 295 B; 2020 / XX75 / 324 A; 3-30 / A/C/C / 194	2213 / XX75 / 236 A; 2215 / XX75 / 267 A; 2117 / XX75,E / 301 B; 2020 / XX75 / 337 B; 3-39 / A/C/C / 210; 4-18 / A/C/H / 226
75-79	2113 / XX75 / 205 C; 2114 / XX75 / 217 B; 2115 / XX75 / 232 C; 2018 / XX75,E / 270 A; 3-30 / A/C/H / 178	2213 / XX75 / 227 B; 2114 / XX75 / 227 C; 2115 / XX75 / 237 A; 2020 / XX75 / 310 A; 3-30 / A/C/H / 186	2312 / XX75 / 235 B; 2115 / XX75 / 256 A; 2117 / XX75 / 301 B; 2020 / XX75 / 324 B; 3-39 / A/C/C / 217; 4-18 / A/C/H / 217	2314 / XX75 / 266 A; 2216 / XX75 / 301 A; 3-49 / A/C/C / 216; 4-28 / A/C/H / 232
80-84	2213 / XX75 / 216 A; 2114 / XX75 / 217 C; 2115 / XX75 / 237 A; 2018 / XX75,E / 270 B; 2020 / XX75 / 297 A; 3-30 / A/C/H / 178	2213 / XX75 / 226 C; 2215 / XX75 / 245 A; 2117 / XX75 / 297 A; 2020 / XX75 / 310 B; 3-39 / A/C/C / 193; 4-18 / A/C/H / 208	2312 / XX75 / 235 B; 2215 / XX75 / 256 B; 2117 / XX75 / 289 B; 2216 / XX75 / 289 A; 3-49 / A/C/C / 206; 4-28 / A/C/H / 223	2413 / XX75 / 260 A; 2315 / XX75 / 292 A; 2219 / XX75,E / 344 A; 3-49 / A/C/C / 216; 4-28 / A/C/H / 232

The chart indicates that more than one shaft size may shoot well from your bow. **Shaft sizes in bold type are the most widely used**, but you may decide to shoot a lighter shaft for speed, or a heavier shaft for greater penetration and durability. Also, large variations in bow efficiency, type of wheels or cams, bow length, string material and release type may require special bow tuning or a shaft size change to accommodate these variations.

The "Shaft Weight" column—indicates shaft weight only. To determine total arrow weight, add the weight of the shaft, point or broadhead, RPS insert, nock and fletching. Where two models are shown for one size, the weight shown is for XX75. Letter codes A-C listed to the right of shaft weight indicate the relative stiffness of each aluminum shaft within that "Shaft Size" box ("A" being the stiffest, "B" less stiff, etc.)

"Shaft Model" column—designates arrow model. XX75 = Gamegetter, Gamegetter II, Camo Hunter, Autumn Hunter and PermaGraphic shafts. E = Eagle Hunter shafts. A/C/H = Aluminum/Carbon/Hunter shafts. A/C/C = Aluminum/Carbon/Comp shafts.

Determining **Actual Bow Weight** or **Actual Peak Bow Weight**. Actual Bow Weight of a recurve bow and Actual Peak Bow Weight of a compound bow can be determined at your archery pro shop.

Although Easton has attempted to consider most variations of equipment, there are other style and equipment variables that could require shaft sizes other than the ones suggested. In these cases, you'll need to experiment and use stiffer of weaker spine shafts to fit your situation.

See page 85 to determine correct arrow length and draw length

SHAFT SELECTION CHART

25½"- **26"** -26½"			26½"- **27"** -27½"			27½"- **28"** -28½"			28½"- **29"** -29½"			29½"- **30"** -30½"			30½"- **31"** -31½"			31½"- **32"** -32½"			32½"- **33"** -33½"		
Shaft Size	Shaft Model	Shaft Weight	Shaft Size	Shaft Model	Shaft Weight	Shaft Size	Shaft Model	Shaft Weight	Shaft Size	Shaft Model	Shaft Weight	Shaft Size	Shaft Model	Shaft Weight	Shaft Size	Shaft Model	Shaft Weight	Shaft Size	Shaft Model	Shaft Weight	Shaft Size	Shaft Model	Shaft Weight

(Detailed data grid of shaft sizes, models, and weights omitted for accuracy.)

If you use one of the following sizes:
2312, 2314 2315, 2317,
2413, 2419, 2512, 2514
with all aluminum RPS insert, add the weight of that insert to your point weight, then subtract 25 grains and re-enter the point weight column within which this adjusted point weight falls.

How to use the EASTON SHAFT SELECTION CHARTS

1. Determine your **Correct Arrow Length** and your **Actual, Actual Peak, Calculated** or **Calculated Peak Bow Weight.**
2. Under the column for recurve or compound bows, locate the box that includes your **Actual, Actual Peak, Calculated** or **Calculated Peak Bow Weight.**
3. Move across the row in a horizontal direction to the right until you locate the column including your **Correct Arrow Length.**
4. One or more recommended sizes are listed in the "Shaft Size" box located where your "**Actual, Actual Peak, Calculated** or **Calculated Peak Bow Weight**" row and "**Correct Arrow Length**" column intersect.

The "Variables" listed below will affect the **Actual Bow Weight** and **Actual Peak Bow Weight** as noted. Combine all the adjustments that apply to your equipment to figure your **Calculated Bow Weight** or **Calculated Peak Bow Weight.**

Variables to the "standard" set-up:

- High Energy Cam – add 10 lbs.
- Dacron String – subtract 3-5 lbs.
- Release Aids – subtract 3-5 lbs.
- Bow efficiency – subtract 3-5 lbs. for older less efficient bows
- Compound bow lengths 44" or less, and draw lengths over 28" – add 4-6 lbs.
- Point Weight – add 1.5 lbs. for every 10 grains your point weighs more than:
  -7% F.O.C. point, aluminum shaft
  -8% F.O.C. point, A/C/C or A/C/H shaft
  -recommended point weight, A/C/E shaft

Reading the EASTON SHAFT SELECTION CHARTS

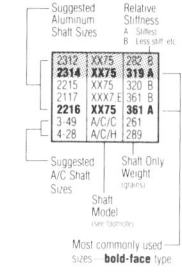

Suggested Aluminum Shaft Sizes — Relative Stiffness A Stiffest, B Less stiff, etc.

2312	XX75	282 B
2314	**XX75**	**319 A**
2215	XX75	320 B
2117	XX75,E	361 B
2216	**XX75**	**361 A**
3-49	A/C/C	261
4-28	A/C/H	289

Suggested A/C Shaft Sizes

Shaft Only Weight (grains)

Shaft Model (see footnote)

Most commonly used sizes – **bold-face** type

C) Determining Arrow Length

Arrow length isgreatly influenced by the handle style of your bow. Over-draw arrow rests on handles with a center-shot tunnel allow the use of shorter arrows. Traditional handle risers with no center shot tunnel require hunting arrows that extend beyond the back of the bow. Shooting a *broadhead* from this style handle means the *arrow must extend beyond the handle riser by at least one-half inch* so the broadhead does not hit the handle or your fingers when the arrow is drawn to full draw. *Field point* equipped arrows need *extend only one-half inch beyond the arrow rest* with this style handle.

Handles with center shot tunnels and a standard rest location can accom-modate broadhead equipped arrows that extend only one-half inch past the arrow rest. Tunnel handles with overdraw arrow rests also require arrows that extend at least one-half inch past the arrow rest. Allow that little extra length so you don't draw the arrow point or broadhead into the arrow rest or into your bow hand when the adrenalin is flowing.

When cutting aluminum or carbon shafts to length, always use a high speed cut-off tool with an abrasive wheel. Such a tool will not bend or distort the end of the shaft. A copper tube cut-off tool or a hacksaw can distort or bend the end of an arrow shaft. Be sure to remove any burr caused by the cutting process. Remember that arrow length is related to arrow spine. The shorter an arrow is cut, the stiffer it will act. Don't be too quick to cut your arrows short. A little test shooting before cutting to final length might change your mind about the length you need.

D) Fletch Selection

Once again, the number, length and type of fletching you need depends upon how you plan to use your arrows. Short range hunting shots and 20 yard target shooting can benefit from larger fletching so the arrow will stabilize quickly. Long range hunting shots and long range target shooting can benefit from short vanes which maintain speed, but that's only part of the picture for hunting shots. Increased speed can produce flatter trajec-tory, but accuracy is the ultimate goal, and there are many more elements than a fast arrow involved in accuracy. Most often, simply having the time to set up and take careful aim at an unalarmed animal can do more for ac-curacy than can any other factor. A fast miss is still a miss, and an arrow too light in mass to have good kinetic energy won't give the needed penetra-tion. An arrow still flying somewhat sideways when it hits the target won't have the desired penetration either. Proper setup and tuning should pre-vent that problem.

Consistent grouping at the maximum distance you intend to shoot is the final determining factor in your choice of fletching. As a rough example, when you need quick stability large fletching (four or five inch vanes or feathers) will do that job well. On longer shots, maybe smaller broadheads and smaller fletching may work well to maintain arrow velocity and accuracy.

Long range target shooting requires small fletching and aerodynamic points. Target arrows with small, light weight points need only 1.75 inch or 2.00 inch fletching to achieve stable arrow flight. Small vanes are great for maintaining down range velocity and accuracy with target arrows, making good grouping at 90 and 100 yards possible. Small vanes lose less velocity but maintain stability since small aerodynamic arrow points are used. By the way, aerodynamic does not necessarily mean light weight, since some target points weigh as much as 125 grains.

E) Point Weight Selection

The weight of the arrow point controls the center of gravity of the arrow shaft. A shaft with no point has a center of gravity located very near the center of the shaft. A light point will move the center of gravity toward the point end of the shaft. Heavier points will move it even further toward the point.

The distance that the balance point lies in front of the center is referred to as F.O.C. (front of center) and is usually given as a percent of the total shaft length. Each size shaft requires a different weight point to create a 10% F.O.C. as shown in Fig. 95. **Each bow and arrow combination may require a different F.O.C. balance point to create the best groups possible.**

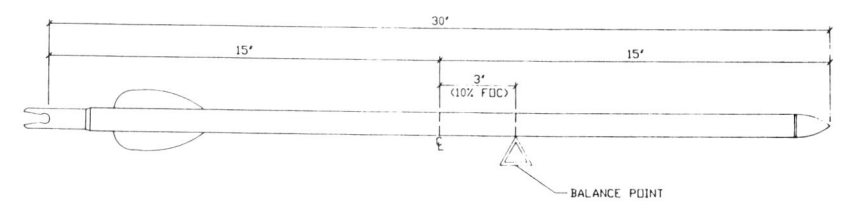

• *Fig. 95. For this 30 inch arrow, a 10% front of center balance point would be located three inches in front of the center of the shaft. For most shafts, this requires a point weighing between 100 and 125 grains.*

Literature supplied by A.F.C. and packaged with their carbon arrows contains a useful formula for calculating the percent F.O.C. for a given point weight. The formula involves the weight, in grains, of the various parts of the arrow, as well as their locations on the shaft. The formula is as follows:

VARIABLES:

A = total arrow length including point and nock
F = total weight of fletching
N = weight of nock
P = total point weight
R = F.O.C. percent in decimal form
W = shaft weight without nock, fletching or point
     (multiply grains per inch by length of shaft)

FORMULA 1: Calculating percent of F.O.C. for a given point weight (P).

$$R = \left[\frac{.5 \times N + 2 \times F + .5 \times A \times W + (A-1) \times P}{N + F + W + P} - (.5 \times A) \right] \div A$$

Rearranging Formula 1 will give Formula 2, which calculates the point weight necessary to obtain a given percent F.O.C. balance. The values obtained will be accurate to within five grains of point weight.

FORMULA 2: Finding point weight for a given percent F.O.C.

$$P = \left[\frac{.5 \times N + 2 \times F - A \times (N+F) \times (.5+R) - R \times A \times W}{(R-.5) \times A + 1} \right]$$

Because a heavy point requires more energy to make it move, the arrow will bend more as thrust is applied to its lighter nock end. This means that heavy points make arrow shafts bend more and act weaker. Lighter points are easier to move, so a given arrow size will bend less when thrust is applied to the nock end. Lighter points make the arrow act stiffer.

Down range accuracy can be affected by small changes in spine caused by small changes in point weight. Twenty or 30 grains of point weight can be the only factor that is keeping your broadheads from grouping at 40 yards or your target arrows from grouping at 80 yards. Trying different point weights while group testing is the only way to find which percent F.O.C. balance point will yield the best groups for a given shaft size.

F) Common Fletching Procedures For Aluminum And Carbon Arrows

Carbon arrows are relatively new on the market and offer some advantages. The other side of the issue is that they require different techniques and procedures to build and tune. Those differences are highlighted in dark type in this chapter.

1) Shaft Preparation

Shaft preparation before fletching is an absolute must. Without a clean surface on the shaft, the glue you use may be totally ineffective. Nothing is more frustrating than getting to a tournament or to your hunting destination and having your fletching fall off.

Several simple steps can take care of this problem, depending upon the type of shaft you use. Aluminum shafts should be scrubbed with Ajax and warm water. Acetone can also be used. Rinse the shafts thoroughly with warm water and dry them with a paper towel. They are now ready for fletching, so do not handle the fletching area.

Carbon arrows should be cleaned with lacquer thinner or denatured alcohol. Acetone used on these shafts may leave residue that will attack the glue you use. An alternate method, which I recommend, is to sand the fletching area of the shaft with very fine sand paper and wipe clean with a dry cloth. This step must be given great attention so a good bond is established between the fletch and the shaft.

2) Nock Preparation

After the arrows are cleaned, twist the nocks snugly onto the end of the shaft. Do not use glue, because after the fletching is complete you will want to remove the nocks and rotate them to their proper position. This position is determined by powder testing — it shows whether the fletching is or is not hitting the arrow rest. When the best possible clearance is obtained with one shaft, glue all the nocks on the shafts in that position.

Carbon arrows require a little more preparation. The last half inch of both ends of a carbon shaft should be sanded with fine sand paper. This prepares the ends for receiving the nock adapter and the point. Wipe these ends with a dry cloth after sanding.

Clean both the nock adapter and the point with alcohol or acetone and glue them to the shaft. Be sure to glue the weight pin into the point before installing the point in the shaft. Use epoxy to insure the best bond. If you plan to use a hot melt glue, be sure to use one with a high melting temperature.

3) Fletch Preparation

Feathers do not usually require any cleaning or other preparation, but vanes do. Most vanes have a residue on them. This residue can destroy the bond between the vane and shaft if it is not removed.

Denatured alcohol is the best agent for cleaning vanes, although acetone can also be used. Place the vane in the glue clamp and wipe the base of the vane with a paper towel dipped in denatured alcohol. Clean all the vanes you intend to use and lay them aside, but do not touch the bases of the vanes.

4) Fletching

The actual fletching of the shaft begins with a test arrow and fletch. With the arrow in the jig and the fletch in the clamp, place the clamp on the jig next to the arrow. Adjust the angle of the clamp so both ends of the fletch will be sure to touch the arrow shaft. Do not place the fletchings in line with the shaft; they must be angled two or three degrees (Fig. 96).

Hunting vanes and feathers should be attached using a curved, helical clamp. The more angle used, the quicker the arrow will stabilize. Check the first fletch that you glue to see if it is angled correctly. Reset the glue clamp if it is not.

Carbon arrows, because of their small diameter and quick recovery, do

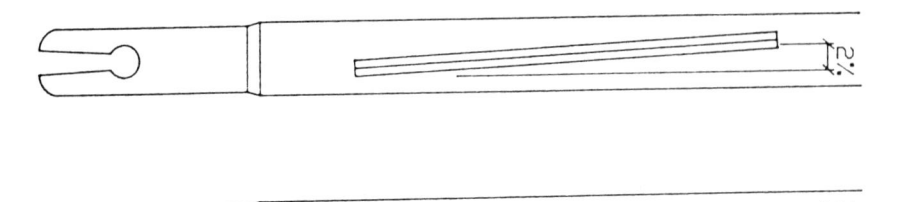

• *Fig. 96. Fletching should always be angled when placed on the shaft. Two or three degrees is normal for aluminum shafts, while one degree is sufficient for carbon shafts.*

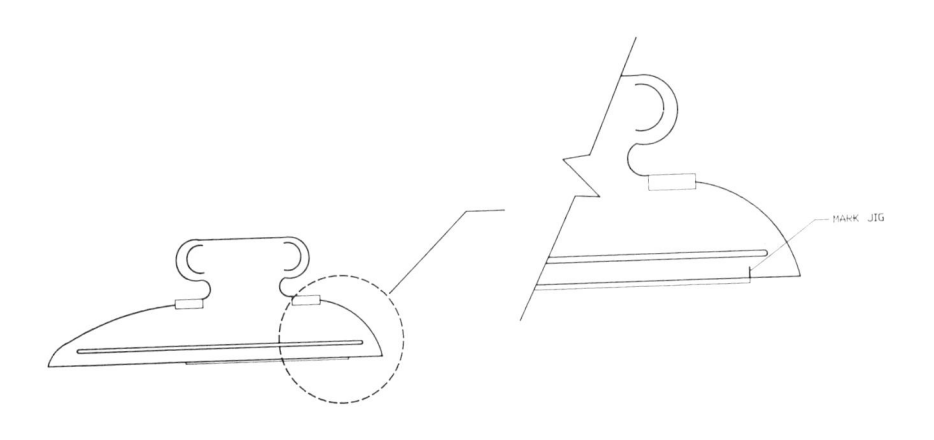

• *Fig. 97. The glue clamp should always be marked at the back edge of the fletch. All of the fletches will then be installed on the shaft the same distance from the nock.*

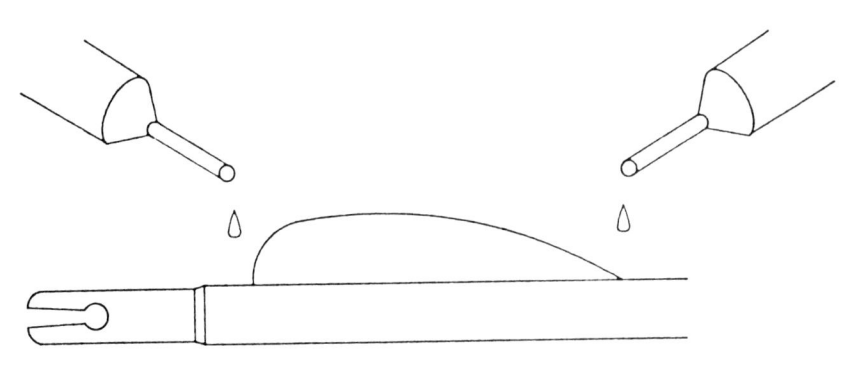

• *Fig. 98. A drop of glue placed on the ends of each fletch will give these vulnerable areas some added protection from damage when the arrow passes through targets and backstops.*

not need as much offset on their fletching. Instead of two or three degrees, one degree offset should be enough. Hunting vanes and feathers should still be attached using a curved, helical clamp.

The type of glue you use for fletching carbon arrows is critical. Some glues do not bond well to carbon. Most instant glues like Super Instant Fletch Tite will bond well but leave little time for adjusting the fletch once it has touched the shaft. Non-instant glues, Saunders for example, will also work well on carbon. Be sure to test the fletching on the first shaft you do.

Before you begin fletching your arrows, mark the clamp where the back of the fletching is to be placed in it, as shown in Figure 97. This will insure that all of your fletches will be placed on the shaft the same distance from the nock.

Begin the fletching by placing a thin line of glue from one end of the fletch to the other. Don't leave any bare spots. This insures that glue will spread between all of the fletch and the shaft when the clamp is placed on the jig.

Next, push the clamp and fletch firmly against the shaft. If you are using a quick drying glue, then don't move it. If you use a non-instant glue, slide the clamp back and forth a little to insure that the glue is spreading evenly between the fletch and the shaft.

Instant cements should be left to dry three or four minutes. Other glues should be allowed to dry ten minutes.

Now, remove the clamp by first opening it and then pulling it away from the shaft. This will prevent pulling the fletch away from the shaft.

Following the fletching of an arrow, be sure to place a drop of glue on each end of each fletch. Gluing each end (Fig. 98) will keep the ends from being pulled away from the shaft when the arrow passes through a target. This extra step will give your fletching job longer life. Allow these drops and your fletching to dry for a day before shooting your new arrows.

5) Point Installation

Once you have selected the point weight for your aluminum arrows, glue the points or inserts into the shaft. First heat the shank of the point or insert, then apply a small amount of hot-melt glue to the point. As you push the point into the shaft, rotate it so the glue spreads evenly around the point and inside of the shaft. Push the point against a board to insure that the point is all the way into the shaft. To prevent smearing the warm glue, allow the arrows to cool before you peel away excess glue on the outside of the shaft.

To remove the point and insert, simply reheat the point, not the shaft, until the point can be pulled from the shaft. Use pliers and a twisting motion for this job on aluminum arrows.

Epoxy glue should be used on the points of carbon arrows. Apply some to the weight pin and the end of the shaft. Push the point and pin straight into the shaft without twisting. Allow the glue to dry for half an hour before removing any excess on the outside of the point or shaft. When it is hard, the epoxy should peel away easily.

Removing the point and pin from a carbon arrow can be done by using low heat on the point but not on the shaft. Low heat will slowly break down the epoxy bond, and the point then can be pulled straight out of the shaft. Again, don't use a twisting motion.

6) Nock Installation

After the point is secure it is time to glue the nock in place. Remove the nock from the end of the shaft. After applying a drop of glue to the end of the shaft, place the nock on the end. Rotate the nock around the end several times so the glue spreads evenly between the nock and shaft.

Align the nock so fletch clearance is at its best. Spin the arrow in your hand to check the straightness of the nock. If it wobbles, realign it and test again until it is straight. Allow the adhesive to set for at least an hour to insure a good bond.

If you use an instant glue, be sure the nock is aligned the way you want it when you push it onto the shaft. You will have little time to rotate the nock after it touches the glued surface.

G) Tuning Aluminum Arrows

The procedure for tuning aluminum arrows is basically the same as the procedure for carbon arrows, which is detailed in the next section. The only difference is in the manner in which point weight is controlled. Carbon arrows have a brass weight pin that can be cut to any length or weight, while the aluminum arrow has only two or three different weight points.

To change the weight of aluminum arrow points, cut the shank of the target point shorter. Field points can be custom made to any weight if you know a machine shop which can do that kind of work.

Another alternative is to leave an extra inch or two on your aluminum shafts. During the group testing phase of tuning you can cut several arrows shorter by 1/4 inch or 1/2 inch increments and retest. After testing different lengths until the arrow is as short as you can shoot it accurately, you should be able to determine the best grouping spine or length.

Keep these ideas in mind while you read the next section on the carbon arrow.

H) Tuning The Carbon Arrow
1) Introduction

Even though carbon arrows are new, proper established tuning procedures still apply. Tuning carbon arrows, like tuning aluminum arrows, involves the following techniques and rules:

a) Final shaft selection done by shoot testing.

b) Nocking point checked by bare shaft testing or by paper testing.

c) Slightly stiff shafts for your bow will shoot better than slightly weak shafts.

d) Longer shaft lengths will act weaker than shorter shafts of the same diameter.

e) Heavier point weights will make a given shaft act weaker, while lighter weight points allow the shaft to act stiffer.

f) Contact between fletches and arrow rest should be avoided.

g) You may encounter glue problems with some vanes on carbon.

2) How The Carbon Arrow Is Different

Carbon shafts are new and different. The main differences are as follows:

a) Smaller diameters.

b) Higher stiffness to weight ratio.

c) Faster arrow speed.

d) Quicker arrow stabilization.

e) Deeper penetration.

f) Different arrow rest requirements.

g) Center shot adjustment of rest requires the cushion plunger or the side plate to be slightly further from sight window of the bow.

h) Fletch angle can be reduced slightly.

i) Nocking point will be slightly lower.

j) Carbon requires different care, certain vanes and adhesives.

3) Tuning Procedure

Select the size shaft indicated as proper for your draw weight and arrow length. Use the AFC comparison chart for carbon versus aluminum and also the Peak Weight versus Arrow Length chart. This is not an exact science for any shaft and is intended to obtain several shafts that will shoot well. Individual bow and shooter characteristics may require a change of one or two shaft sizes to get optimum results. When in doubt, choose the slightly stiffer shaft size.

Cut the carbon shafts one inch longer than the aluminum arrows you have been using. The extra length will help compensate for the greater stiffness of the carbon shaft and allow experimenting by removing 1/4 inch segments to observe spine and grouping changes.

Your arrow rest must be altered so it will support the smaller carbon arrow while allowing fletch clearance. The side plate or cushion plunger will need to be further from the side of the bow since the carbon arrows are smaller in diameter. Check the clearance with white powder foot spray. No vane or feather should be contacting the rest. A launcher style rest with a narrow point launcher should work well for release shooters. Finger shooters should try an A.T. Olympiad or a Cavalier T300 with a Flipper II or similar rest combinations.

The nocking point location for carbon arrows will be about 1/16 to 1/8 inch lower than for the larger aluminum arrows. Start tuning about 1/8 to 3/16 inch above level. This should allow the shaft to be level.

The brass or stainless steel weight pin used in the arrow points can be cut to obtain an F.O.C. (front of center) balance point of 7% to 11%. Measure the arrow length from the bottom of the nock throat to the tip of the point. Calculate 7% to 11% of the length and mark your arrows that far in front of the center of the shaft. Cut the balance pin to obtain the desired balance point.

You may want to start tuning with two fletched and two non-fletched arrows and a full length weight pin. Bare shaft test or group test as you cut the balance pin shorter. This would assure finding the balance point which produces best grouping.

Target arrows should be fletched using 1.75 inch or 2.00 inch straight vanes placed on the shaft with a one degree offset. You can also try 1.75 inch or 2.9 inch spin-wing vanes.

Hunting arrow preparation would require using the brass balance pin or the heavier stainless steel balance pin. The total pin and point weight should be approximately the same as the broadhead you intend to use. Four-inch vanes or feathers should provide adequate stabilization for most broadheads on carbon arrows. You can reduce the angle of helical curve used since the carbon tends to recover quicker than aluminum.

Most finger shooters begin bare shaft testing at approximately 15 feet and continue out to 30 feet. Adjust your nocking point so the bare shaft is entering at about the same height as a fletched shaft. Adjust the point and pin weight so bare shafts enter nock left (for right handed shooters) with heavy points but tend to enter straighter as point weight is reduced. Group test from long range with each point weight. Shaft length can also be altered to gain the desired bare shaft result.

Most release shooters begin paper testing at about 10 feet and continue to about 30 feet. The nocking point should be set so the nock end of the arrow is tearing a near perfect hole or testing straight high or high left (for right handed shooter) no more than 3/4 inch.

Begin with the full length weight pin that gives an 11% F.O.C. balance, using at least three arrows. Paper test as you reduce point weight by cutting 1/4 inch sections from the pin. Also group test from long range as point weight is reduced. By the time you have cut your three experimental arrows as short as you dare shoot safely, you should know what point weight groups the best.

Broadhead testing begins with field points about the same weight as the broadhead you intend to use. Use the paper testing procedure. You may try altering point weight if you are not locked into using a given weight broadhead. To get good results, you may have to change to a different point weight or to a different shaft spine. At this point, you should employ the tuning steps mentioned in an earlier chapter.

Chapter 10

Serving, Repairing and Making Strings and Cables

One of the most common repairs that a compound bow needs involves the string. Center servings need to be repaired or replaced, end servings come loose or separate, and strands break in the string itself. A serving tool and knife are all you need to make the necessary repairs.

If you prefer to make your own strings, you might want to invest in a string jig. Having one can reduce the costs of strings and cables considerably and also shorten the time it takes to replace them. I can make a new string in about 15 minutes, put it on the bow and install the serving in another 15 minutes, and be ready to shoot in an hour. Cables take a little longer because you have to make two of them, but making your own is a real time and money saver.

Following the process laid out in this chapter, you can learn to make a good string after only a few tries. One important point: be sure to keep the string tight on the jig for all steps. I'll start you off with a method for installing servings, since the beginning and ending techniques for those apply to all finish and end steps for making strings and cables.

The Center Serving

The center of the bowstring should be served with either monofilament or Polygrip braided serving thread. I use monofilament in size #18 or #20. A 12-strand DynaFlight string with #18 mono serving will fit the ACC .088" nock well. The #20 mono is thicker and will fit nocks with wider throat sizes, as will strings of more strands.

Another combination that I can give you as a rule of thumb applies to the bigger uni nocks on aluminum arrows. Indoors, I shoot the 2413 XX75 shaft with the Super Nock system. That nock fits well on a 14-strand 450 Premium (from BCY Fibers) string with #18 monofilament for center serving.

My first recommendation is to **install any NEW string on the bow before doing the center serving**. If you're repairing an old one, leave it on the bow and fasten the bow in a press or some type of holding device so you can remove the old, damaged serving from the string.

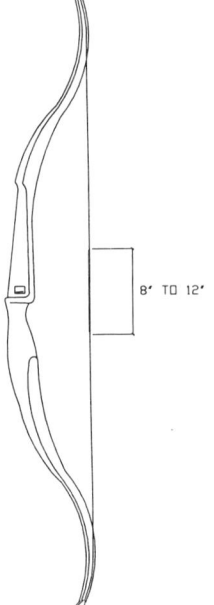

• *Fig. 99. When you install a new serving, place at least three inches of it above the nocking point. Eight or nine total inches of center serving should be sufficient to protect the string where it may rub your arm or cable guard. If you have frayed string below the nocking point, use more than nine inches to cover it.*

8′ TO 12′

When you install the new serving, place at least three inches of it above the nocking point. This will prevent the serving from slipping up the string under the pressure of your fingers or release aid. Eight or nine total inches of center serving should be sufficient to protect the string where it may rub your arm or cable guard. If you have frayed string below the nocking point use more than nine inches to cover it. You may have to remove the cable guard to do this.

You may want to start serving near the cable guard and serve up the string to three inches above the nocking point. This method doesn't require removing the cable guard unless you want to serve lower than that.

In any case, the following steps for serving a string can be followed. You will have to practice them several times, especially the "finish" steps.

Strings & Cables

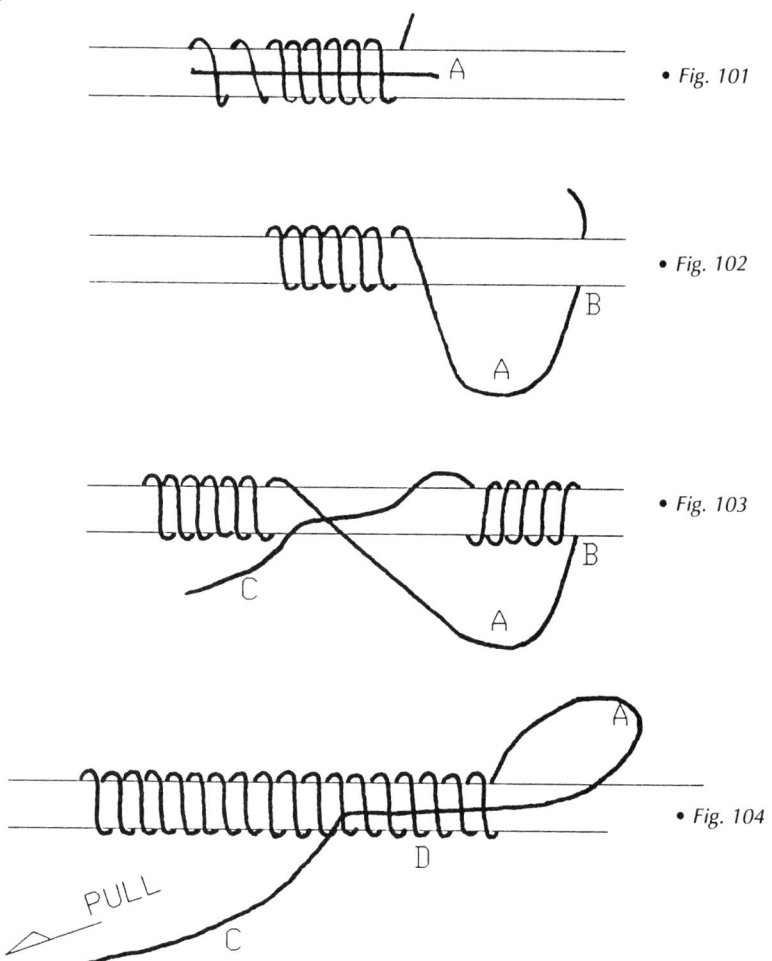

• Fig. 100. Use two four-inch pieces of arrow shaft with nocks on both ends to separate the strings from the cables.

• Fig. 101-104. Read the steps in The Actual Serving Process at the bottom of this page and on page 100.

• Fig. 101

• Fig. 102

• Fig. 103

• Fig. 104

The Actual Serving Process

Begin the serving process by separating the strings from the cables. I use two four-inch pieces of arrow shaft with nocks on both ends, as shown in Figure 100.

Next, place the end of the serving thread between the strands of the bowstring about three inches above the nocking point, allowing a loose end to lay downward along the string (end A in Figure 101). Serve down the string and over top of that loose end for about one-fourth inch before pulling the end until it is snug. Continue serving until you have one to 1-1/2 inches of serving over the loose end. Now pull the loose end out of the way — it can be cut off later — and continue serving the desired distance down the string.

The finish step can be done using only the serving tool if you follow these steps:

a) Keeping tension on the serving, pull out about 12 inches of serving to form loop A in Figure 102;

b) Hold it at the middle and loop the serving tool back to the bowstring several inches away from where you last served (point B in Figure 102);

c) Continue wrapping serving inside the loop you just made but back toward the original section of serving. Wrap in the same direction around the string as before, creating one-half inch or more of auxiliary serving (B in Figure 103);

d) Now lay several inches of serving thread C along the original portion of serving as shown in Figure 103;

e) Holding the big loop tightly, continue wrapping the original portion of serving by hand, keeping even tension at all times. As you continue to increase the length of original serving you will wrap over thread C in Figure 103;

f) As the original serving (D in Figure 104) increases in length, the auxiliary serving will unwrap until all that remains is the 12-inch loop A in Figure 104;

g) Now pull the serving tool from point C (Figure 104) until the 12-inch loop is pulled through and under the last one-half inch of original serving. Snug and cut off the serving thread to finish.

Nocking Point Installation

When you have completed the center serving, install your peep sight and nocking point locator. A good starting location for the nocking point is 1/4 inch above the level of the arrow rest. This will allow the bottom of the arrow to sit level when it is mounted on the string and rest.

Many professional archers I know use a nock locator made with knotted serving thread. This type can be turned like a nut on a bolt to adjust it up or down the center serving. It adjusts but doesn't slip under pressure from below. My favorite material for this is BCY Polygrip serving thread; it has tremendous durability.

The knotted locator can be tied onto the bowstring using the following steps:

a) Tie one overhand knot of serving thread onto the bowstring at the desired location (Figure 105);

b) Pull the two loose ends of the nylon to the back of the bowstring and tie another single overhand knot below the first knot (Figure 106);

c) Bring the ends of thread to the front of the bowstring and tie knot 3 above knot 1 (Figure 107);

d) Moving from front to back and up the bowstring, tie knots 4 through 9, leaving knot 9 loose;

e) Use a separate eight-inch piece of bowstring material to form a pull-through loop which you can push up through knot 9, then snug knot 9 (Figure 108);

f) Tie knot 10 on the back side of the bowstring and slip the loose ends of the serving through the pull-through loop in front;

• Fig. 105-108. Read the steps for nocking point installation beginning on page 100 and concluding on this page.

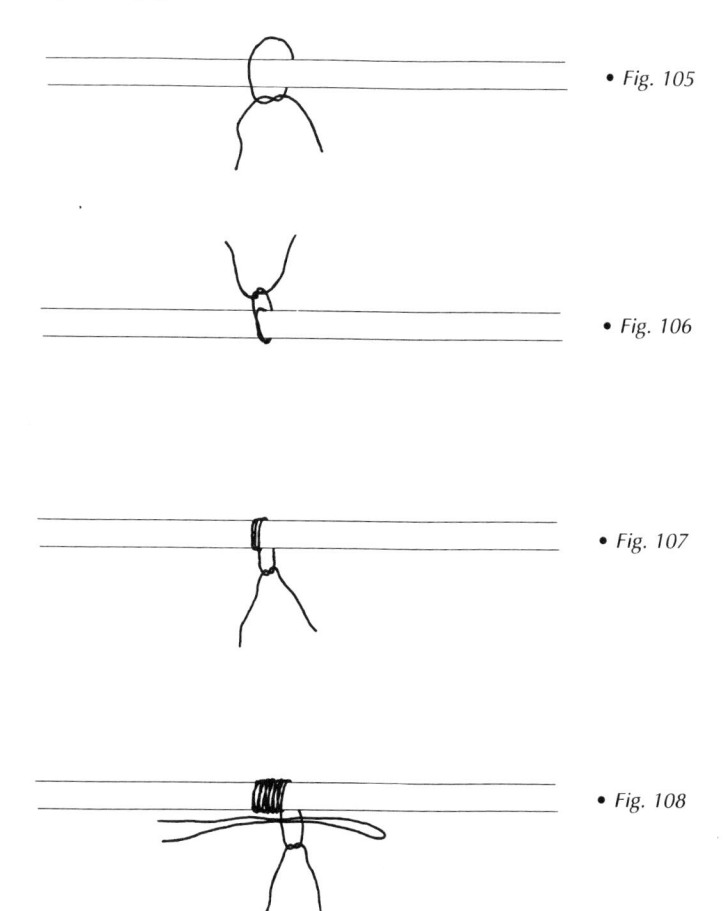

• Fig. 105

• Fig. 106

• Fig. 107

• Fig. 108

g) Now pull the pull-through loop in order to get the serving ends down through and under knot 9;

h) Pull the ends of the serving thread tight and cover the entire set of ten knots with fletching cement and allow to dry at least one hour. Trim any excess serving with nail clippers.

The resulting knotted nock set can be twisted around the center serving like a nut on a bolt. This will make it easy to find the nocking point location you feel yields the best groups of arrows in the target. **You may want to place one below the nock of the arrow since many of today's short bows and small nock combinations allow the nock to slip down the string during the power stroke of the bow.** These knots will not dig into the nocks like the metal rings sometimes do and will give consistent accuracy for thousands of shots.

A highly popular nock locator these days is the rope loop. Figure 109 shows a simple way to install a loop. I find it best to use a rope without a core, or a rope with a core made of the same material as the shell. I use a 5-1/2-inch piece, melt the ends to form beads, then tie it to the string. I also tie on knotted nock locators above and below the rope loop to make sure it doesn't slip up the string.

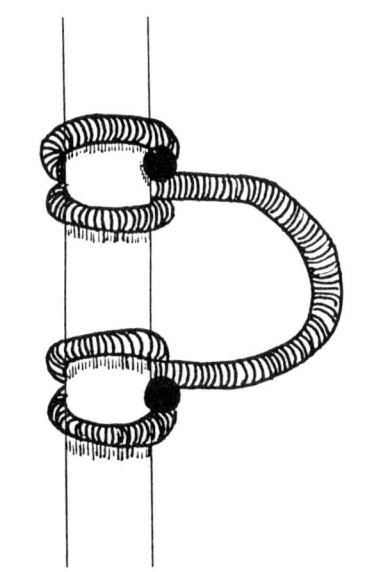

• *Fig. 109. A rope loop like this is a popular nock locator because it is secure and reliable. Instructions to make one are given in the paragraph above this.*

Peep Installation

Any peep sight you decide to use should be installed so that an **equal number of strands is on each of it's sides.** If not, it will be offset from the string center and may not ever roll around to your eye consistently.

Many archers I know tie their peeps into the string using the ten-knot process described for nocking points. This can be done above and below the peep. When the knots are tied tightly they can be pushed up and down

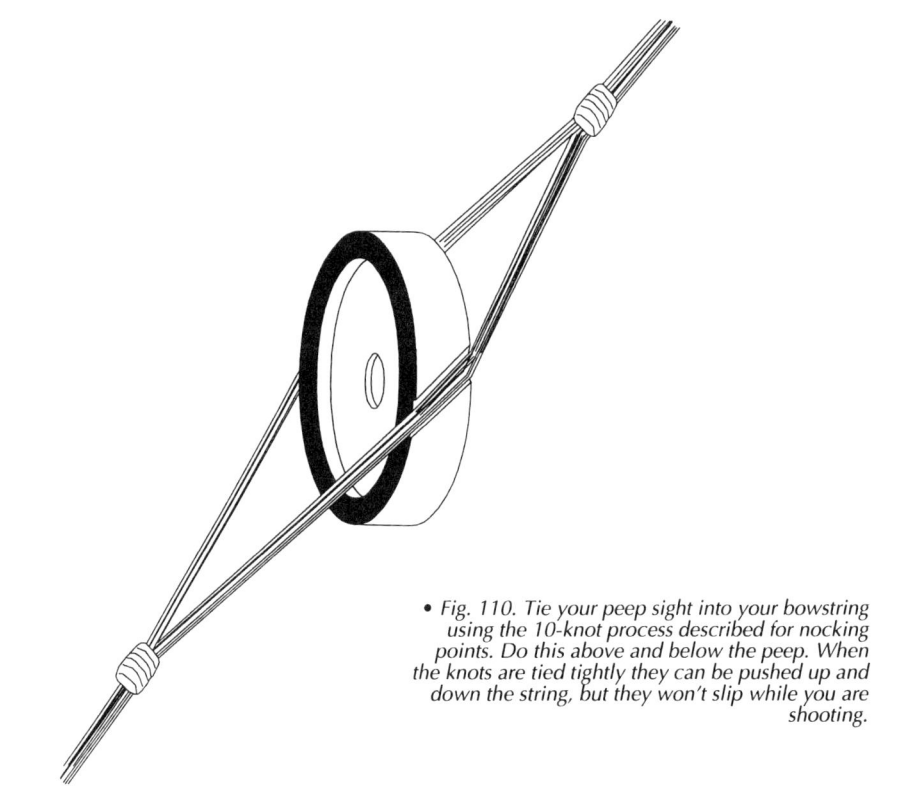

• *Fig. 110. Tie your peep sight into your bowstring using the 10-knot process described for nocking points. Do this above and below the peep. When the knots are tied tightly they can be pushed up and down the string, but they won't slip while you are shooting.*

the string, but they won't slip while you are shooting. I do this for all of my own bows, sliding the knots to within an inch of the peep (Figure 110). This method gives great long term results with no slipping.

The second advantage of the ten-knot method is that it allows you to adjust the peep so it rolls to your eye for every shot. When the peep isn't rolling to your eye, just slide the knots away from the peep and move one or more strands of the bow string from one side of the peep to the other. Keeping the same number of strands on each side, continue adjusting until the peep rolls correctly to your eye. Don't forget to slide the knots back to within an inch of the peep when you finish adjusting.

End Servings

Repairing an end serving on a bowstring can be done using the same techniques needed to install the center serving. The beginning and ending processes are the same for all servings you'll have to do.

Building Your Bowstring

There are many good ways of making and serving a bowstring. The method outlined in the following pages is the one I use for all of my own strings. I trust it to give me the best strings that can be made, either by hand or by machine. Follow it and you'll get a good string after only a few tries.

The Purpose of the Bowstring

The job of the bowstring is two-fold. First, it must transfer energy from the archer's arms and back muscles to the limbs of the bow. Next, it must transfer that same stored energy from the limbs to the arrow. This energy transfer gives the arrow speed and direction.

The string's job is much like that of the baseball bat, hockey stick or golf club: it acts as a facilitator to transfer energy. It must do it repeatedly with a very high degree of consistency for a long period of time. If it doesn't, it's no good to anyone.

The string you build must have the proper protective coverings, called servings, in the proper places so that excessive wear won't damage it. Your string must also have the correct number of strands to match your nocks and draw weight, and it must be the correct length. The center serving must be the correct diameter so your arrow nocks snap easily on and off, allowing accurate shooting. Paying close attention to all these details will help you build a reliable, long-lasting bowstring.

Choosing Your Bowstring Material

Today there are several choices of materials for making your own strings. One is a material called Dyneema, which is marketed by several companies. BCY Fibers calls their most recent version DynaFlight 97. The other common material is a blend of Vectran and Dyneema; the BCY version is called Premium 450+.

Both materials work well and each has its strong point. The pure Dyneema string has a high resistance to abrasion, but under extremely high loads it will "creep" in length. The blended material doesn't stretch and doesn't fray.

Either string material can be twisted to increase strength or to decrease the length of the string. **Shortening the string to adjust draw length on the compound bow is a common adjustment; just don't try to shorten the string more than a quarter of an inch.** Remember, too, that shortening the string on a recurve bow will increase it's draw weight.

Selecting the Number of Strands

The number of strands needed in a bowstring depends on the peak weight of the bow and the nock size used. High peak weight requires more strands, but more strands require wider nock throats. A compromise must be struck. Both the draw weight and nock fit must be satisfied through the choosing of the number of strands and the size of the center serving material. If your nocks don't fit properly, you might have poor arrow flight and bad groups.

Usually a 14- or 16-strand DynaFlight string, which should fit a 9/32-inch nock, is used on a 50- to 60-pound bow. The same nock can be used on a 12- or 14-strand Premium 450+ string with good results, since this material has a slightly larger diameter. I use 12 strands of DynaFlight or 10 strands of Premium 450+ for my ACC nocks with the .088-inch throat slot. I have to add two or four strands to shoot the Super Uni nocks on large aluminum arrows.

Most compound bows with cam-shaped wheels require strings with more strands. The added strength helps to withstand the extra forces that a cam applies to the string. To avoid long term stretching or "creeping", use a blended material like the BCY Premium 450+.

Regardless of the number of strands you choose, select the nock size that fits the string properly. Proper fit will allow you to pull the arrow off the string using two fingers and only a slight tug on the arrow. If the nock fits too tightly, poor flight and bad groups are the result.

Measuring String Length

The length of your bowstring should have been stated in the manufacturer's specifications literature which came with the bow. If you don't have that literature, remove the string from the bow and measure it from tip to tip. **This length is the stretched length of your string and not necessarily the length of the string when it was manufactured.** It may have been 1/4 to 1/2 inch shorter when it was made, since some strings stretch a little when first put on the bow, or it may have been twisted many times and is now shorter than when it was made.

If you have no specs available and the old string is broken, place the bow in your bow press and bend it until the appropriate axle-to-axle distance is reached. Judge this by other bows with similar handle and limb length. Use a piece of string to make a model bowstring, then measure the model. Test the new string you make after Step Two of the building process by putting it on the bow to see if it is the appropriate length. If it isn't, you haven't lost a lot of time and material, so just start over.

The String and Cable Building Process

The building process is four steps:

1) Layout — The strands that form the string are looped around four posts and the ends are tied fast.

2) Loop serving — The end loops of the string are formed by serving a two- to three-inch section on each end of the string.

3) End serving — The loops are closed by placing the string on two

posts and serving around all strands for four to 12 inches.

4) Center serving — The center section, where the nock of the arrow is placed, is served while the string is on the bow. This insures serving tightness.

The String Jig

Like any job, building a bowstring can be done best when the proper tools are used. In this case, a good string jig is required to get good results. The jig need not be expensive, but it does need to be strong enough to stay in place while being used.

As mentioned earlier, four posts or pins are required to build a string. These posts must be stationed the correct distance apart so the finished string will be the desired length. The posts must be movable so they can be stationed in line, as well as in a rectangular formation.

Commercial string jigs will probably do the best job. Look for a jig that is made of metal, is easy to adjust and is not too large to store. The pin mounts should pivot on axles which can be locked into the positions needed for string making.

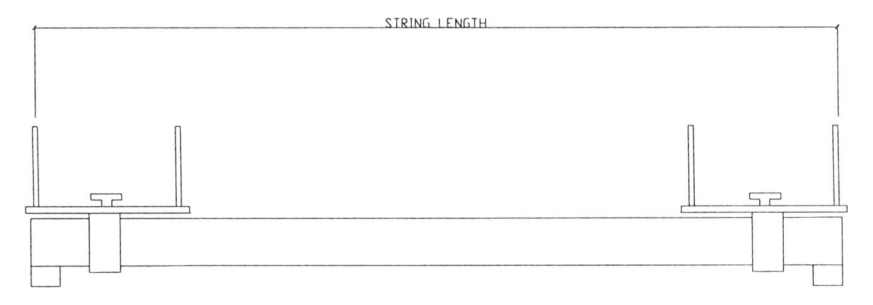

STRING LENGTH

• *Fig. 111. Position the four pins of the jig so they form a straight line. Set the distance between the outer pins to match the length of the string you wish to make.*

Step One: STRING LAYOUT

Begin the layout of the bowstring by clamping the string jig to a table top tightly enough that the jig cannot move during the string making procedure. Now position the four pins of the jig so they form a straight line (Figure 111). Set the distance between the outer pins to match the length of the string you wish to make.

At this point you must remember to make any compensation in length for the stretching of the string after it is installed on the bow or for the twists you may want to add. Maybe the jig you have allows the jig pins to pull closer together as you wrap string around them, and you have to add a little length to the initial setting. Here is where experience will tell you what to do. Keep that in mind as you learn to make strings. Keep notes on each string's finished length and how far apart you set the pins.

Rotate the pin mount bars 90 degrees (Figure 112). This will allow the pins to form a rectangle about which the loops of the string may be wrapped.

Begin by fastening the end of the bowstring material you have chosen to pin A. A clove hitch knot works well. Now wrap the first strand around pins B, C, D and back to pin A. This completes your first loop. Continue making loops like this until you have the number you want. Remember, 10 loops will fold together to make a 20-strand string (my example in this case). You may need a different number of strands for your string or cables, so proceed accordingly.

When you have completed the number of loops you desire, tie the end of the last loop to pin B. Leave several inches extra and cut. You now have 11 strands between A and B but only 10 at the other end.

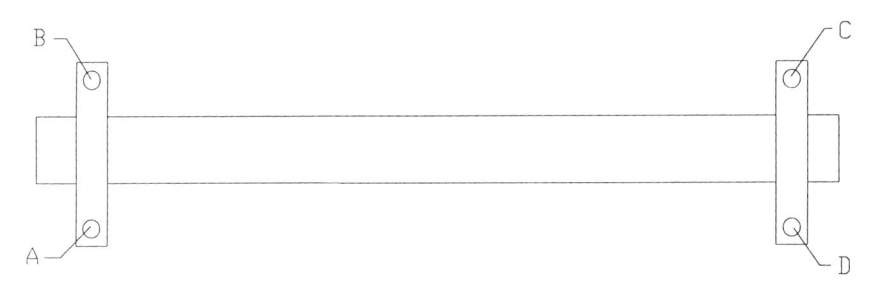

• *Fig. 112. Rotate the pin mount bars 90 degrees. This will allow the pins to form a rectangle about which the loops of the string may be wrapped.*

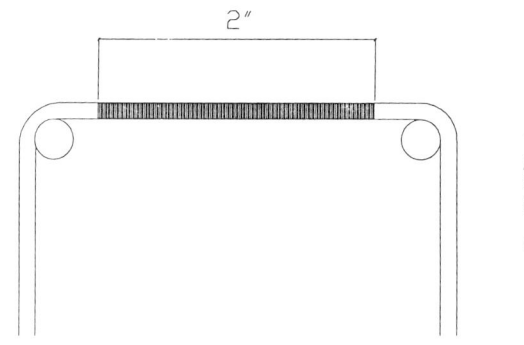

• *Fig. 113. Without moving the jig pins, wrap two inches of serving on either end – between pins A and B and between pins C and D. Two inches is sufficient to make a one-inch loop on a finished string.*

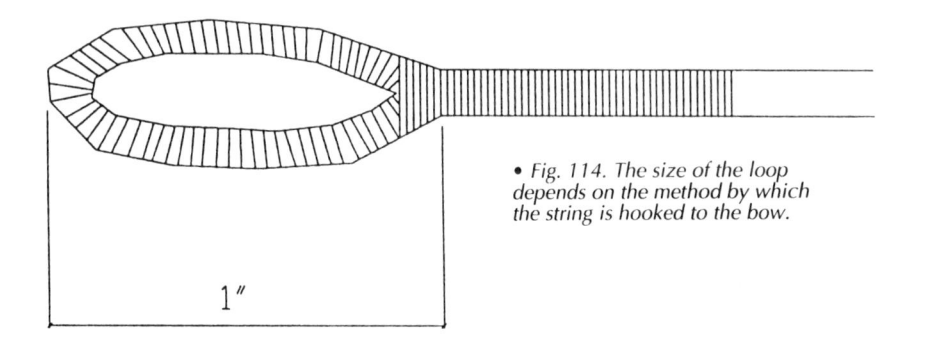

• *Fig. 114. The size of the loop depends on the method by which the string is hooked to the bow.*

1"

Step Two: THE END LOOP

Without moving the jig pins, wrap two inches of serving on either end — between pins A and B and between pins C and D (Fig. 113). Two inches is sufficient to make a one-inch loop on a finished string. Be careful to serve in the middle of each section or, as I do it, start two inches from pin A on one end and two inches from pin C on the other. Then when you reset the jig for Step Three, the served portions will be at exact opposite ends.

The size of the loop depends on the method by which the string is hooked to the bow. Recurve bow limb tips require a bigger one- to 1-1/2-inch loop. Steel cable anchors require a loop length of three-quarter inch to one inch. A small loop of one-half inch can be used on strings that attach directly to a pin on the compound eccentric wheel.

The loops and ends of your strings and cables should be served with a material such as BCY Polygrip serving thread or BCY #2-D serving. These materials take a beating and stay in place if you install them using a good serving tool with tension control.

The Actual Serving Process

Begin between pins A and B. Place the end of the serving thread between the strands of the bowstring about two inches from pin A. Now serve toward B and over top of that loose end for about one-half inch before pulling the end until it is snug. Trim off any excess and continue serving until you have 1-1/2 inches of serving.

The finish of the serving can be done using only the serving tool if you follow the steps outlined in the preceding section on center servings.

Step Three: THE END SERVING

The end serving completes the loop and adds a protective wrap to the last four to 12 inches of the string. The serving length depends on how much of the string wraps around the wheels. Bigger cams have a larger circumference and require more serving.

To do this, the jig pins must be placed in-line. In fact, only the two inside pins need to be used to stretch the 10 loops of string into a 20-strand bowstring.

The two inches of loop serving installed on either end should each be hooked around a pin. Be sure to stretch the string tight before locking the jig in position. It's not only easier but better to serve over a tight string.

Using the same serving thread and method as before, begin serving at the ends of the loop serving. Some shooters like to overlap some of the loop serving as an added protection. After some experimenting, you can decide for yourself which method you like best. I prefer to serve over about 1/4-inch of the loop servings to take advantage of the extra protection.

• *Fig. 115. The end serving completes the loop and adds a protective wrap to the last four to 12 inches of the string.*

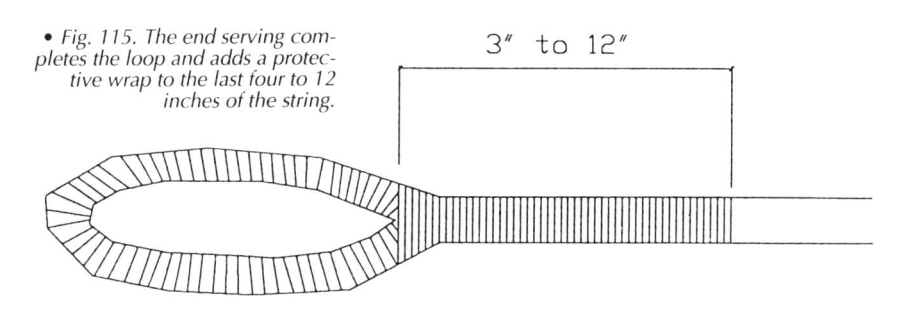

3″ to 12″

Strings for recurve bows need about three inches of end serving while compound strings need quite a bit more. The strings and cables for a compound wrap around the wheel and require four to 12 inches of end serving. The exact amount depends upon the eccentric wheel size you are using. Nine inches works well for my 2-1/2 inch wheels. Smaller wheels will require less, while most big cams take more.

Step Four: CENTER SERVING

The finish steps are the same as described in the center serving section. In fact, any time you want to finish a segment of serving or repair a loose end, use those steps. In the field, your can use this technique to repair a loose end by hand with just a few wraps.

Install the string on the bow before doing the center serving. Once again, follow "The Actual Serving Process" instructions, tie on some nock and peep locators and you're set for lots of trouble-free shooting.

NOTES:

Chapter 11

Twenty Most-Asked Questions About Compounds

Through the course of an average year, I am asked many questions about tuning compounds. Most of the time they fall into the list that follows. I have supplied brief answers in this section. The text of this book provides more detailed answers for all questions.

1. Should the draw length on my bow be the same for shooting with my fingers as it is when shooting with a release aid?
No. Most archers need to set the draw length of their bows one to two inches longer when shooting with their fingers.

2. On multiple draw length wheels and cams, does any one draw length setting perform better than another?
On many bows the short draw setting performs better, but experimental data suggests that this is not the case on all bows.

3. What is the best arrow rest for the compound bow?
Because the action of the eccentric wheels of the compound imparts up and down motion to the arrow, a rest which provides some vertical flexibility as well as horizontal flexibility is necessary.

4. Do bows perform better when set at their maximum draw weight?
Most compounds are more efficient in the middle of their weight adjustment range, but best overall performance and grouping may occur anywhere in the weight adjustment range. When set at their maximum draw weight, the limbs of compounds will have more pre-bend, which is a desirable condition.

5. Does changing draw weight affect draw length?

When weight adjustment is made by using weight adjustment bolts in the butt end of the limb, draw length is not affected. Eccentric rollover will not be affected by weight bolt adjustment, but weight adjustment made with a cable guard or idler wheel repositioning will change draw length.

6. What results can I expect if I shoot my compound from the wall?

Inconsistent arrow flight and erratic high and low arrows will result.

7. What results can I expect if I shoot from in front of the valley?

Erratic high arrows and a tendency to creep before releasing the arrow will be the result.

8. How should I set the tiller on a two wheel compound?

Set the tiller measurements anywhere you like. Changing tiller on a two-wheeler will only change the handle angle between the limbs and will not affect how much one limb will work relative to the other limb.

9. Is there a difference between tuning a wheel bow and a cam bow?

No. You must, however, be more particular when adjusting the draw length on a cam bow.

10. Should I use a 1/8-inch nocking point on a compound bow?

No. Most compounds will shoot better with the nocking point set in the range of 3/16-inch to 6/16-inch.

11. Should I use a bare shaft or a fletched shaft when paper testing?

I recommend a fletched shaft whose fletches are clearing the arrow rest.

12. What tear holes are best when using the paper test?

Most finger shooters and release shooters look for a paper tear which shows the nock end tearing high and left for a right hander and high right for a left hander.

13. What should I do if one fletch continues to strike the arrow rest as proven by powder testing?

Many times a simple rotation of the nock on the shaft will eliminate one fletch striking the rest.

14. What is the best nock fit?

Your nock should snap on the string, but you should be able to pull it off with a slight tug using the index finger and thumb. If the nock fit is too tight, you need bigger nocks or a string with fewer strands.

15. Do feathers work better than vanes?
Feathers will stabilize an arrow quicker than vanes of equal size. Feathers also are more forgiving.

16. Should I use right wing or left wing helical curve on my fletching?
Use either, but make sure all of your fletching is the same on all of your arrows. Do not use fletching which is straight down the shaft.

17. Should I line up my broadhead blades with my fletching?
As long as your broadhead point is mounted straight on the shaft, you will see no difference in flight when altering blade alignment.

18. Should broadheads and field points shoot the same?
No. Points of different weight and configuration will very seldom have the same point of impact on the target, or the same flight characteristics.

19. Should I sight in my hunting bow with the bow quiver installed?
Yes. Any weight added to one side of the bow will change the point of impact of the arrows.

20. Should I sight in from my tree stand?
If you plan to hunt from a tree stand, then sight in from one, but also know where those sight pins will shoot from level ground.

21. Should I get more penetration from a faster, light arrow or from a slower, heavier arrow?
Experimental data shows that a heavier arrow will have more energy than a light arrow shot from the same bow. Therefore, the heavier arrow will give you better penetration.

22. Why does this chapter have the title ''Twenty Most Asked Questions,'' when in fact it has 22 questions?
Nobody's perfect. Good luck, good arrow grouping, clean flight, tournament trophies and filled tags.

Paper Test Guide

Instructions
  When the nock end of the arrow tears in any of the eight directions shown, then make a combination of the indicated adjustments.

Right Hand Shooter
(left hand shooter must reverse left/right adjustments)

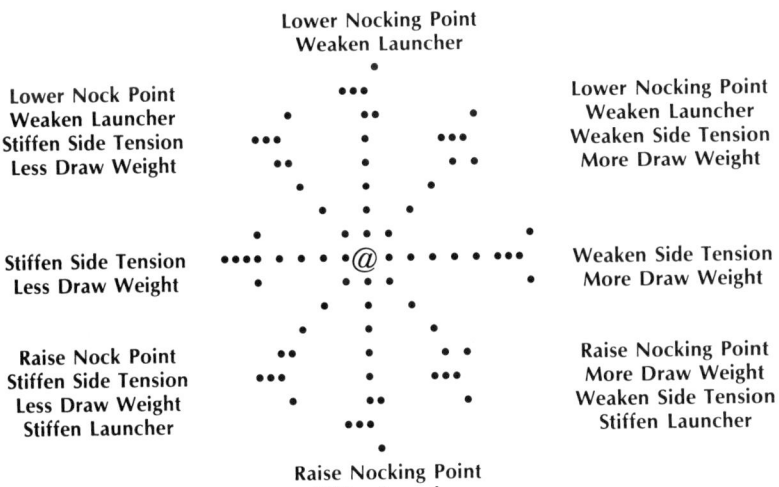

Lower Nocking Point
Weaken Launcher

Lower Nock Point
Weaken Launcher
Stiffen Side Tension
Less Draw Weight

Lower Nocking Point
Weaken Launcher
Weaken Side Tension
More Draw Weight

Stiffen Side Tension
Less Draw Weight

Weaken Side Tension
More Draw Weight

Raise Nock Point
Stiffen Side Tension
Less Draw Weight
Stiffen Launcher

Raise Nocking Point
More Draw Weight
Weaken Side Tension
Stiffen Launcher

Raise Nocking Point
Stiffen Launcher

BOW FACT SHEET

Owner _____

Manufacturer _____

Model _____ Serial Number _____

Recurve _____ Longbow _____ Compound _____

Two-Wheel _____ Four-Wheel _____ Two-Cam _____

Riser Material: Wood _____ Magnesium _____ Aluminum _____

True Draw Length: With finger tab _____

With release aid _____

Traditional Draw Length: With finger tab _____

With release aid _____

Peak Weight at Your Draw Length _____

Compound Bow Holding Weight in the Valley _____

Pounds of Let-Off (peak wt. hold wt.) _____

Percent Let-Off (pounds of let-off / peak wt.) _____

Tiller Measurements: Top Limb _____

Bottom Limb _____

Static Tip Deflection (pre-bend): Top Limb _____

Bottom Limb _____

Brace Height _____ Nocking Point Height _____

String Length _____ Number of Strands _____

Distance of Peep Above Nocking Point _____

Limb Type: Wood _____ Laminated Fiberglass _____

Laminated Fiberglass w/ Wood Core _____

Fiber Reinforced Plastic _____

Tuning Fact Sheet

Date _____

Bow Brand _____ Model _____

Peak Weight _____ Hold Weight _____

Arrow Size _____ Arrow Length _____

Field Point Weight _____

Broadhead: Weight _____

Number of Blades _____

Blade Angle: Straight _____ Left _____ Right _____

Nock Size _____ Number of Strands in Bowstring _____

Fletching Type: Feathers _____ Vanes _____

Number of Fletches _____ Length of Fletches _____

Angle of Installation: Right _____ Straight _____ Left _____

Right Helical _____ Left Helical _____

Arrow Rest: Brand _____

Type: Shoot-Around _____ Shoot-Through _____

Mount Position: Standard _____ Overdraw _____

Nock Fit: Good _____ Tight _____ Loose _____

Initial Nocking Point Location _____

Note: Nocking point location is the distance above a line which extends at a 90-degree angle from the bowstring and lies on the arrow rest. This location is measured to the **bottom** of the nocking point locator, with the arrow nocked **below** the nocking point locator. Thus, the nocking point height also can be defined as the distance to the top side of the arrow nock as it is nocked in the position defined here.

Field Point Testing

Powder Test: Contact _____ No Contact _____

Adjustments _____

_____

Paper Test: Nock End is Tearing   (High)   (Left)
(Level) and (Center)
(Low)   (Right)

    Adjustments _____

    _____

15 YARDS: Arrows in Gold = _____ (Goal = 6 of 9)

      Others   = _____

25 YARDS: Arrows in Gold/Red = _____ (Goal = 6 of 9)

      Others   = _____

45 YARDS: Arrows in Gold/Red/Blue = _____ (Goal = 6 of 9)

      Others   = _____

Adjustments: Nocking Point _____

             Centershot _____

             Rest Tension _____

             Arrow Size_____

             Draw Weight _____

             Draw Length _____

             Others _____

             _____

NOTES:

NOTES:

The "On Target" Series
of Outdoor / Shooting / Hunting Books

UNDERSTANDING WINNING ARCHERY, by Al Henderson, coach of the 1976 U.S. Olympic Archery Team, international coach and shooting consultant. Mental control means easier archery gear set-up, more-productive practices, and winning archery – for target, field and hunting shooters. ISBN: 0-913305-00-6. Library of Congress Catalog Card Number (LCCN): 82-074190. TCC (Target Communications Corporation) Book #01-001; $9.95.

TAKING TROPHY WHITETAILS (2nd Edition), by Bob Fratzke with Glenn Helgeland. In-depth, detailed information on year-round scouting (and its huge payoff), scrape hunting, rut hunting, late season hunting, camo, use of scents plus entire new chapter on mock scraping and licking branches. Learn why this consistent trophy-taker says, "I spend 90% of my time in the woods scouting and 10% hunting." ISBN: 0-913305-02-2. LCCN: 83-050905. TCC Book #01-003; $10.95.

TO HECK WITH GRAVY wild game cookbook, by Glenn and Judy Helgeland. Gourmet results from quick, easy recipes. Includes 209 recipes (roasts, steaks, marinades, soups/stews, ground meat, fish and birds), plus meat field dressing tips, handling and/processing tips, spice chart, low-sodium diet tips and more. ISBN: 0-913305-05-7. LCCN: 85-179767. TCC Book #01-005; $12.95.

TASTY JERKY RECIPES FOR EVERYONE, by Glenn and Judy Helgeland. Spicy, mild, sweet and no-sodium recipes for three different meat cut thicknesses and tenderness. Make in oven, smoker, dehydrator or microwave. Book #01-006; $2.00 plus stamped, addressed #10 return envelope.

TUNING YOUR COMPOUND BOW (3rd Edition), by Larry Wise, the recognized master at understanding and interpreting the mechanics of compound bows. New material includes round wheel, single cam and super cam set-up and tuning chapters, making/serving/repairing strings and cables. Basic info includes pre-use bow preparation, draw stroke, power stroke, shooting from the valley, fine tuning, test shooting, tuning the Fast Flite cable system, building and tuning aluminum and carbon arrows. ISBN: 0-913305-15-4. TCC Book #01-008; $11.95.

TUNING & SILENCING YOUR BOWHUNTING SHOOTING SYSTEM (3rd Edition), by Larry Wise. Problem-solving information on fitting the bow to your body style and shooting form for consistent best results; broadhead effects on arrow flight; noise reduction throughout the entire system; aiming and shooting strategies; proper practice; plus tuning the Fast Flite cable system, building and tuning aluminum and carbon arrows. New material includes round wheel, single cam and super cam set-up and tuning chapters, making/serving/repairing strings and cables. ISBN: 0-913305-16-2. TCC Book #01-009; $11.95.

TUNING & SHOOTING YOUR 3-D BOW, by Larry Wise. Explains the 3-D archery game and who shoots it; arrow speed – the 3-D advantage; 3-D archery and bowhunting. Detailed information on choosing the right equipment, the force-draw curve of a cam, choosing and tuning 3-D arrows, shooting your 3-D bow. Practice strategies for 3-D and for bowhunting, and shooting 3-D competition. ISBN: 0-913305-10-3. LCCN: 92-83910. TCC Book #01-010; $10.95.

BECOME THE ARROW (the Art of Modern Barebow Shooting), by Byron Ferguson with Glenn Helgeland. Details the "become the arrow: philosophy; walks you step-by-step through that shooting system; explains how to visualize arrow flight path and sight picture; shooting from practice and mental exercises (and discipline); how to develop the necessary focus and concentration; tuning for barebow shooting; bowhunting details on moon phases and other advanced items; most-commonly asked questions, building a longbow. ISBN: 0-913305-09-X. LCCN: 92-83909. TCC Book #01-011; $12.95.

MUZZLELOADING FOR WHITETAILS & Other Big Game, by Toby Bridges, the nation's foremost black powder hunter/writer. Black powder technology and rifles have changed dramatically the past ten years with the introduction of the percussion in-line style. More and better black powder hunting seasons now are the big draw. Here's the most up-to-date technical data on black powder rifles (new and traditional) and accessories, plus detailed, no-nonsense black powder hunting tips. ISBN: 0-913305-12-X. LCCN: 94-49359. TCC Book #01-012; $12.95.

STEPS ALONG THE HUNTER'S PATH (Volume 1). A new kind of book. Based on seminars given by some of today's finest deer and turkey hunters at the five 1998 Deer & Turkey Expos produced by Target Communications in Michigan, Illinois, Ohio, Wisconsin and Tennessee. This book greatly expands that material into a wealth of hunting information, offering the combined wisdom of literally a "who's who" of expert hunters in the country. Also includes complete trophy contest winners' lists from all five of the 1997 Deer & Turkey Expos; county by county trophy information – what was taken and what it was taken with; more than two dozen venison recipes; listing of the Outdoor Photo Contest winners (with photos) from all five 1997 Expos; how/where to get your trophy scored and entered in record books, and more. ISBN: 0-913305-14-6. LCCN: 97-52714. TCC BOOK #01-014; $19.95.

SHIPPING & HANDLING — $2.75   All prices (books and s/h) are in U.S. funds.
Wisconsin residents add 5.6% tax.

SEE YOUR DEALER
or order directly from the publisher.
(MC/VISA accepted)

Write or call for a FREE catalog:
TARGET COMMUNICATIONS CORPORATION
7626 W. Donges Bay Rd., Mequon, WI 53097
414-242-3990 • 1-800-324-3337
www.deerinfo.com

About The Publisher....

TARGET COMMUNICATIONS

TARGET COMMUNICATIONS produces Deer & Turkey Expos in Illinois, Michigan, Ohio, Tennessee and Wisconsin. The company also publishes, in its "On Target" series, books on deer hunting, archery, muzzleloading and wild game cooking.

A new series — "Steps Along The Hunter's Path" — is an 'added value' book, published annually in a new volume, complementing and adding valuable how-to tips and details to the deer and turkey hunting information and trophy deer data learned at the Deer & Turkey Expos.

GLENN HELGELAND

Target Communications' President Glenn Helgeland was editor of *Archery World* magazine (now *Bowhunting World*) 11 years — 1970-1980. He is the founding editor of *Archery Retailer* magazine (now *Archery Business*). He has been a columnist for *Bowhunting World, American Hunter, North American Hunter* and *Archery Business* magazines. His hunting and natural history articles have been published in the above publications, plus *North American Whitetail, Field & Stream, Outdoor Life, Sports Afield, Bowhunter, Bow & Arrow Hunting,* plus state publications.

He was the Editor of the Pope and Young Records Book, 2nd Edition; co-author, with John Williams, men's 1972 Olympic archery gold medalist, of the book "ARCHERY FOR BEGINNERS," and author of the "COMPLETE BOWHUNTING" book for the North American Hunting Club.

Helgeland was Associate Editor of *NATIONAL WILDLIFE* magazine 1968-1970.

He has won awards for his writing and publishing from the National Shooting Sports Foundation and the National Archery Association.

Helgeland is an individual member and past director of the Outdoor Writers Association of America (OWAA). His company is a supporting member of this same organization.

Target Communications is a member of the National Association of Consumer Shows (NACS) and the International Association for Exposition Management (IAEM).

122